Sustainable Quality

Sustainable Quality

Joseph Diele

BUSINESS EXPERT PRESS

Leader in applied, concise business books

Sustainable Quality

First published in 2021 by
Business Expert Press, LLC
222 East 46th Street, New York, NY 10017
www.businessexpertpress.com

ISBN-13: 978-1-95334-962-0 (paperback)
ISBN-13: 978-1-95334-963-7 (e-book)

Business Expert Press Supply and Operations Management Collection

Collection ISSN: 2156-8189 (print)
Collection ISSN: 2156-8200 (electronic)

First edition: 2021

10 9 8 7 6 5 4 3 2 1

Description

Times have changed and the concept of using quality as a competitive advantage has been diminished or even lost completely. Quality only becomes a competitive advantage when it is embraced by the entire company.

It is not that there is a lack of quality improvement models. There are many available, such as: ISO, Baldrige, Total Quality Management, Lean, Six Sigma, to name a few. While all these models have been successful, why has there not been one model that takes hold as *the* model? Why do improvement efforts seem to fizzle out? Why are they not sustainable? Why are continuous improvement efforts not continuous?

Something has been missing from the strategy, planning, and implementation of these quality efforts. That missing ingredient has been culture.

This book lays out both a strategy and the practical tools and methods needed for sustainable quality, without comprising on either. The book presents a new quality model. This new model explains why building a positive culture is a prerequisite to real quality improvement. Building on a strong culture, the book shows how to develop the right tools, methods, and training to keep everyone engaged.

Transformation requires a clear and inspiring vision. However, the way people react to any change has everything to do with the culture and environment they are working in. Continuous improvement means change. Change happens through people. All the best tools and training will not be successful (especially over the long term) if a true culture of quality has not been established first.

Keywords

quality; sustainable quality; leadership; culture; cost of quality; continuous improvement; functional quality; TQM; change management; quality strategy; profitability; process; data analysis; data-based decisions; teams; new quality model

Contents

Foreword

I met Joe Diele about 26 years ago at StorageTek, a data storage company founded in 1969 later acquired by Oracle with a focus on large-scale tape libraries. I was a director building a new development organization, and I needed to ensure quality and reliability from the earliest stages of defining the product architectures and designs. I had heard about this engineer that was touted as one of the best reliability and quality engineers in the company, and so I did what any good director would do and recruited Joe to join our team. Joe more than lived up to the amazing reputation he had built at StorageTek and recruiting him was truly one of the smartest things I've done. Joe exuded passion and ability unlike any quality engineer I had ever met, and with his help, we implemented some of the best quality processes I've ever had the privilege of being associated with.

Why is quality important? When you have created a culture of quality, you will bring functional products to market faster, you will achieve greater customer satisfaction and market penetration, you will enjoy improved profitability as a result of reducing your non-conformance costs, and you will improve employee job satisfaction by creating a culture of excellence. Quality cannot be an afterthought—it must become part of the team culture through cultivated intentional practice. That is what makes this book *Sustainable Quality* a must-have for any development or quality assurance team member or manager. And that is why I was honored when Joe asked me to write this forward for his book. It will help you to achieve a new level of success.

I can assure you this book *Sustainable Quality* will become one of your most valued "go to" books. You will find no shortage of books that speak to tools, technologies, and processes to track quality metrics and administer quality tasks. What makes this book unique and powerful is its focus on how to bring a culture of quality and excellence into your company. It has been my experience, all the greatest tools and methods will not matter if you don't have a culture that embraces quality, change and a real dedication to improvement. Make no mistake this will be one of the key challenges you will have. Joe has done a good job throughout the book, addressing key factors to help you influence what a healthy culture can and should look like in preparation of establishing a culture of Sustainable Quality. The question is, what are you going to do with that information? By embracing the value of continuous improvement, quality and excellence, you will take your team and company to new heights of success. But engagement requires commitment. As the leader, that commitment must start with you.

—Fred Casanova

Preface

Working in Quality my entire career, I have had the opportunity to see firsthand what the impact can be when successfully implemented. Not only within the companies I have worked at. This also includes companies I have worked with closely, such as suppliers, partners, customers, and even some competitors. Being successful with quality, and more importantly sustaining that level of quality, is easier said than done. It is my belief, that culture is the critical factor in whether quality efforts fizzle out or truly achieve continuous improvement. In fact, culture is a critical factor for any business success.

Much has been written about culture and how it can make or break a company. Yet so many companies today are either unaware or unwilling to create the type of culture that elevates their business. When your business is dealing with high absenteeism or, worse, high turnover, it should be no surprise that you are also dealing with a high cost of poor quality. You might not recognize it as a quality cost, but you are likely struggling with excessive waste, low productivity, and repeated mistakes.

The intent of this book is not to be a technical book on statistics and quality control. This is really a book about management for the future, with the sole purpose of raising your business to a whole new level. And by new level, I am specifically talking about being more profitable. It is my strong belief, and thus the reason for writing this book, that a better understanding and appreciation of quality and its direct correlation to culture will help you achieve that.

This book will not give you a step-by-step procedure on how to get there. The truth is nobody can provide that to you. Every company is different, each with its own set of issues and needs. This book is more about creating awareness of what real quality looks like. It is not a test team checking a product for defects, or inspector sorting good products from bad or a support team handling a customer complaint. It is about evolving beyond those types of activities. I am hopeful that you will get a

better view, a more wholistic view, of how quality can influence your suppliers, thrill your customers, and save you time and money along the way.

We will touch on many areas within a typical business, with thoughts
and suggestions about how each area can be improved. But make no mistake. The real value, the actual payoff, comes from putting all the pieces
together and cashing in on the synergistic impact of quality that can only
be realized collectively across the entire business, fueled by a culture that
embraces continuous improvement.

Acknowledgments

While I have been fortunate in my career to have worked with and for some exceptional people, there have been three managers that had a dramatic impact on my career and life in general. Their guidance and support are very much appreciated.

Joe Lovato showed me early in my career that leading people was more effective than directing people. It was his mentorship that put my career on a course toward constantly examining how I could become a better leader.

Bob Wood always had such great insight on business, products, and processes. He is exceptional at getting you to think and look at things differently. He could talk in depth across a range of subjects like nobody I have ever met. I have always enjoyed each opportunity to visit with Bob and I know that I always walked away a little smarter after talking with him.

Fred Casanova pulled me out of thinking day-to-day and encouraged me to be more creative, take chances, and build visions. Then he would back me up and support me 100 percent of the time. Fred taught all of us that worked for him that is was ok to have fun at work. He would set a high bar but then lead by example. Fred had a true gift for leading people. He would genuinely create the feeling that you were missing out if you did not follow. To say that we went through some challenging times together would be an understatement. However, I could not think of anyone I would rather be side by side with than Fred.

I am so blessed to have three beautiful daughters, Angel, Talia, and Jonina. I am so proud of each of you, for what you have already achieved and know that you are just getting started. You each inspire me to always do the right thing and set the right example. You are the joys of my life.

To my amazing wife, Tammy. You changed my life the day I met you and have given it meaning every day since. You simply make me a better man.

CHAPTER 1

Introduction

The Impact of Quality

Quality Saves Money

What if, with relative minimal investment, your company was able to save between 20 and 30 cents of every dollar it earns or increase revenues or market share by like proportions? This isn't a rhetorical question; rather what is attainable if one improves the quality of the product or service they deliver. By eliminating poor quality and increasing good quality, companies save money and improve their bottom line.

How much could you save if you did *everything* "right the first time"? If you *knew* that everything was done right, you would not need to spend time (and money) on: inspecting, re-inspecting, design changes, bug fixes, testing, retesting, reworking, scrap, troubleshooting problems. You also would not need dedicated staff that deals with irate customers, complaints about poor service, product issues, or incur all the costs associated with returned products or service calls.

It is not unusual for companies that do not measure their cost of poor quality (COPQ), to be spending as much as 30 percent of sales on poor quality activities. That means that one and one-half days per week, you are redoing work that was not done right the first time. How much could you save if you cut that down to one day per week? How about four hours per week? Or, one hour per week?

We will discuss cost of quality (COQ) and cost of poor quality (COPQ) in more detail later in the book. For now, you should know that quality costs are split into four categories: prevention, appraisal, internal failures, and external failures.

An example may help put this into perspective. Let's say a business made $30 million in revenues last year. If their COPQ was really at 30 percent, they would be spending $9,000,000 per year or $750,000 per month to do things over. If you reduced the COPQ from 30 percent down to 20 percent, they would be *saving* $3,000,000 per year or $250,000 per month. Ideally, you would like to have COPQ down below 10 percent.

Let's explain that 30 percent a bit further. The 30 percent attributed to poor quality would be divided between internal failures and external failures. For a typical technology company, this might include costs such as the following:

Internal Failure Costs

- Time spent on failure analysis of failed products resulting from internal testing, including engineering and manufacturing tests
- Scrap and rework of products that failed internal testing
- Engineering changes due to internal test failures
- Retesting of product that was previously tested.

External Failure Costs

- Support costs due to a customer failure
- Cost of product(s) returned due to a customer failure
- Failure analysis of customer issue
- Engineering changes due to a customer failure
- The logistics costs of sending replacement product and returning failed product
- Lost or deferred sales due to customer frustration.

While making improvements for these types of issues are not easy, they are possible. And, who does not want to reduce costs and improve margins? For some businesses, saving time is more important than saving money. Doing things right the first time is always faster than doing things over.

What Is Quality?

What exactly is quality? Dictionary.com defines quality as "an essential or distinctive characteristic, property, or attribute."

What has always fascinated me about quality is that most of these key principles can be used across any industry (e.g., technology, health care, government, restaurants, large corporations, and small businesses). These principles are very transferable. While there are industry differences, in terms of regulations, standards, and certainly products and services, most quality best practices can be adapted (with some minor customization) to any business.

There are many definitions of quality. Some are very specific like the definitions from three of the most well-known quality experts.

W. Edwards Deming:[1] Never-ending improvement of the extended process for which management is responsible.

Joseph Juran:[2] Quality is fitness for use.

Philip Crosby:[3] Quality is conformance to requirements.

The definition of quality is often in the eye of the beholder. A simplistic view of quality may be that it provides a level of awareness for how good or bad a product or service is, whether measurable or not.

I would define quality as meeting the customer's expectation. Although a simple definition, it needs to be unpacked to be fully understood. Meeting customer's expectations means not only do you know what they need, but also know what they expect (not always the same thing). It means you have the structure, controls, and resources in place to ensure those expectations are consistently met. Furthermore, I believe there is an essence of quality, an inward nature, that is equally important, if you want quality to be sustainable. I think of this intrinsic nature of quality as a continuum of pride and perfection. Therefore, even when it is not perfect, you are driven, based on pride, toward continued improvement. You continue along that continuum to make it better as you strive for perfection.

---

[1] Gitlow and Gitlow (1987).
[2] Juran (1951).
[3] Crosby (1979).

When you are deeply committed to what you are doing and who you are doing it for, you have that inner determination to build your product or service to the absolute best of your ability. That happens when you are working in an inspiring and supportive environment. It is more about the people doing the work and how much of their heart and soul they put into the final outcome. The outcome can be a completed product or a set of completed steps that then gets passed on to the next person to add their own contribution toward a completed product or service.

For technology companies, quality can be used as a benchmark to compare similar products or services. When I worked at Fusion-io, we had developed the first enterprise level solid state storage (SSD) device. As the newcomer to enterprise storage, we had to compete against the large industry leaders that had a long history of selling hard drives (spinning disk) for enterprise storage. Because it was a new technology, our messaging about the quality and reliability of SSD became a critical success factor. Fusion-io went on to be highly successful in the enterprise space, in no small part because that messaging got through.

There is often this notion that quality adds cost to a product or to a company. The truth of the matter is that it depends. If you are consistently having to repeat work that was previously done because it was not correct the first time, then improving quality is an added cost. If you do not have enough trust in your people and processes such that you need to add a screen that searches for defects (inspecting or testing), those appraisal costs do add up. However, if you shift your focus toward preventing defects before they happen, you are avoiding the costs and time associated with reacting to failures and most likely reducing the time and costs associated with searching for defects.

Product and Process Quality

There are two considerations when discussing quality improvement. There is product quality and process quality.

Product Quality

Product quality is the level of outgoing quality delivered from your process. Said another way, it is what your customer expects to see. Considerations for product quality include the emphasis on quality in your design, the verification and validation, manufacturing, and final packaging. Product quality emphasizes the level of outgoing quality to ensure it meets the expectations of your customers. Does the final product comply with the stated requirements, specifications, and regulations? Is it a product or service your customers want?

Process Quality

Process quality is the level of consistency built into the steps and tasks associated with creating, building, testing, and shipping your final product. It is about repeatability. Considerations for process quality include instructions, procedures, and metrics for the key tasks, such as requirements analysis, design activities, test activities, supply chain and logistics activities, and support activities. Process quality is focused on the efficiency and effectiveness of getting these tasks completed consistently. You want to understand what the variance is in your key processes how you can reduce it. Variance can be introduced in a number of ways, such as differences in people, tools, or parts. What are your key processes? Are they repeatable? Are there measurements in place? Does everyone involved understand their role and deliverables?

Both product and process quality are important when you are looking at quality improvement. You cannot focus on one without the other. The approach to each is slightly different. We will discuss these further in later chapters.

Quality Improves Profitability

There are two primary ways to improve profitability: (1) increase sales and (2) improve margins, shown in Figure 1.1. Better quality can certainly lead to increased sales, through enhanced customer satisfaction, making more competitive products, and increased name recognition. But quality has a direct impact on margins that can be measured. This includes: (1) reducing costs with more efficient processes and more reliable products and (2) increasing value by removing waste and doing things right the first time.

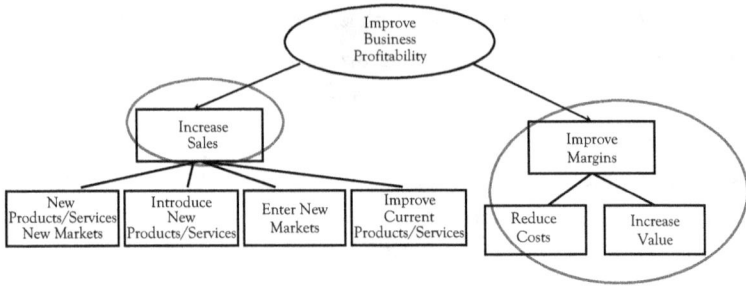

Figure 1.1 Improve business profitability

Increase Sales

Improve Quality to Increase Value

Think about building quality into your designs, which means designing the right product at the right time at the right price. Juran called this quality by design (QbD). Or use the voice of the customer (VOC) to convert customer feedback into requirements. Really understand what value you are providing.

Value goes beyond feature and function. Make their ordering process easy and simple. Reduce their wait time. Make access to your products and services convenient. Make all interactions with your customers hassle-free and painless.

Map out your customer interactions for inquiries, orders, returns, and complaints. Identify possible points of delay or frustration and eliminate them.

Improve Quality to Increase Market Share

The Ansoff product/market growth matrix,[4] shown in Figure 1.2, is a planning tool used to analyze and generate four alternative directions for the strategic development of a business or corporation. Using quality as your differentiator, you can strategically position your product into the four quadrants.

---

[4] Spencer (2013).

Ansoff Matrix

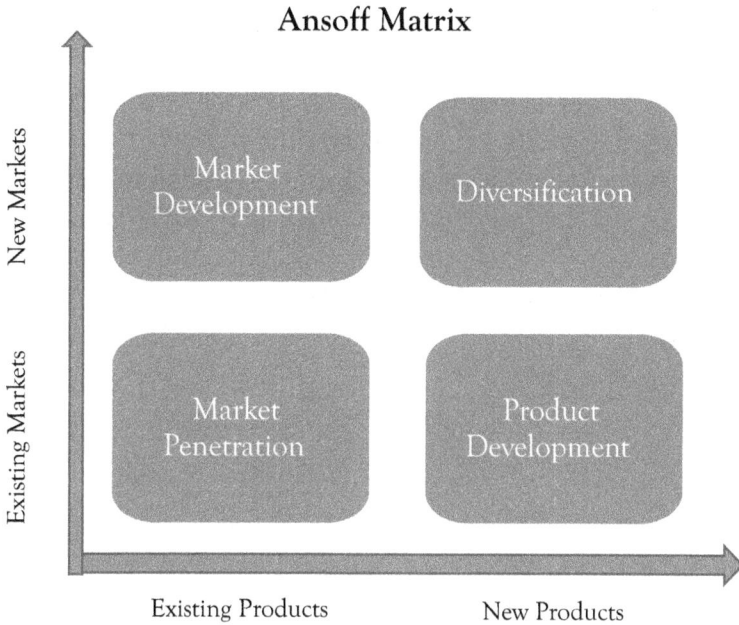

Figure 1.2 Ansoff matrix

The four strategies of the Ansoff matrix are as follows:

1. *Market penetration*: The focus is on increasing sales of existing products to an existing market.
2. *Market development*: The focus is on entering a new market using existing products.
3. *Product development*: The focus is on introducing new products to an existing market.
4. *Diversification*: The focus is on entering a new market with the introduction of new products.

Of the four strategies, market penetration is the least risky while diversification has the most risk.

Market Penetration

In market penetration strategy, the organization tries to grow using its existing offerings (products and services) in existing markets. Specifically, it tries to increase its current market share in its current market. This can be achieved by selling more products or services to established customers or by finding new customers within current markets. Typically, the company pursues increased sales for its present products in its present markets through more aggressive promotion and distribution. This strategy works in a growing market, where simply maintaining market share will result in growth.

Market penetration can be accomplished by:

- Price decrease
- Increase in promotion and distribution support
- Minor product refinements

From a quality perspective:
- Reducing waste and the cost of poor quality allows you to lower price
- Building a reputation for high quality will help in promotional activities
- Understanding the voice of the customer (VOC) will help identify product enhancements that attract more customers.

Market Development

In a market development strategy, the company tries to expand into new markets (geographies, countries) using its existing offerings with minimal product/services development. This strategy is more likely to be successful when

- the firm has a unique product technology it can leverage in the new market;
- it benefits from economies of scale if it increases output;
- the new market is not too different from the one it has experience of; and
- the buyers in the market are intrinsically profitable.

This can be accomplished by identifying different customer segments:

(a) Selling in different geographical areas (new countries/regions)
(b) Selling through different sales channels (e.g., online)
(c) Selling to different demographic groups (e.g., by age or gender)

Options (a), (b), and (c) may be entirely new to the company and this poses a risk. However, if the company holds a large market share for the specific product type, or has strong brand recognition, or a strong brand range, then this strategy could work in its favor.

From a quality perspective:

Different countries/regions may have different requirements (e.g., certifications, laws). Well-defined requirements are essential to eliminate surprises that can derail a launch.

Collaboration with new channels and groups will require well-defined processes and procedures, as well as clear roles and responsibilities to ensure all involved are aligned.

Product Development

In product development strategy, a company tries to create new products and services targeted at its existing markets to achieve growth. This involves extending the range of products available to the company's existing markets. This may be a good strategy for a company that already has a strong market share of a specific market and wishes to diversify its product range. However, it would need strong research and development capability.

These products may be developed by:
- additional investment in research and development;
- acquisition of rights to produce someone else's product;
- buying someone else's product and rebranding as your own; and
- joint development with ownership of another company who need access to the firm's distribution channels or brands.

From a quality perspective:
- Developing and acquiring new products will require a solid understanding of the voice of the customer (VOC).
- When buying or having someone produce a product for you, your requirements need to be clearly defined. Don't just focus on features and functions. Define your standards for quality and reliability as well.

Diversification

In diversification, an organization tries to grow its market share by introducing new offerings into new markets. This strategy has the most risk because both product and market development is required. It is best to use this strategy when it can be a supplement to the existing core business. The diversification can be organic but often happens from the result of an acquisition or merger.

Beyond the opportunity to expand your business, the main advantage of diversification is when one business might suffer from adverse circumstances, another may not be affected.

From a quality perspective, diversification makes quality improvement more complex. It becomes more about insisting on the right culture and standards of quality as you grow through acquisitions, partnerships, and expanding your own workforce.

Improve Margins

One way to improve margins is to reduce costs. An effective way to reduce costs is to utilize the Lean principles that focus on eliminating waste. Lean is a set of principles and tools that was developed by Toyota in 1988. We will dive deeper into Lean and reducing costs in later chapters. But for now, here are the eight types of waste identified in Lean principles. To help improve margins, you should look for opportunities to reduce waste (which saves time and money) by focusing on these eight areas.

1. *Defects*. Products or services that do not meet specification and require additional resources to correct.

2. *Overproduction*. Producing too much of a product before it is actually needed.

3. *Waiting*. Time spent waiting for the previous step in the process to complete.

4. *Nonutilized Talent*. Employees that are not effectively used or under-utilized in the process.

5. *Transportation*. Transporting items or information that is not required to perform the process from one location to another.

6. *Inventory*. Inventory or information that is sitting idle (not being processed).

7. *Motion*. People, information, or equipment making unnecessary motion due to workspace layout, ergonomic issues, or searching for misplaced items.

8. *Extra Processing*. Performing any activity that is not necessary to produce a functioning product or service.

Where Has Total Quality Gone?

Today the emphasis on quality is just not as strong as it once was. Having worked in quality for many years, I always find it interesting when talking to friends, family, and new acquaintances in casual gatherings. If you tell someone you work in finance, engineering, sales, hospitality, or nursing, they immediately have a general idea of what you do. But if you tell someone you work in quality, you usually get a response like, "Hmm, ok. So, what exactly do you do?" Classes on quality are not a typical option in most curriculums. That is not to say there are not quality classes available, but you'll need to do some searching to find them. Quality is just not a typical career path that most college students think about.

All companies say they want quality. But most companies just do not understand that everything you do has an impact on quality, either positively or negatively. To fully recognize the impact quality can have, it needs to be taught or coached into every company function and every person within those functions. Today, any knowledge of companywide quality is passed down on the job from one generation to the next, at least at companies that understand its value. With this in mind, a brief historical view of quality might establish some context for the following chapters.

During the first international quality management conference in 1969, Armand Feigenbaum would first use the phrase *Total Quality Management* (TQM).[5] Kaoru Ishikawa would later indicate during the conference that TQM should apply to all employees within the organization—from the workers to the head management.

In the United States, quality really came to the forefront through work and teachings of Joseph Juran and W. Edwards Deming in the 1970s and 1980s. It is hard to mention Juran and Deming without mentioning their mentor, Walter Shewhart. Shewhart was a leader in the quality movement during the first half of the twentieth century. His mentoring of engineers at Western Electric and his groundbreaking work with control charts arguably led the quality revolution and launched the quality profession. He developed the often-used improvement cycle Plan-Do-Check-Act (PDCA), also known as the Shewhart cycle.

The modern quality revolution began in the 1970s, when the quality of Japanese goods surpassed those of the United States and Europe. The United States had to change to stop the imbalance and began to place a big emphasis on quality improvement in the 1980s.

In the 1980s, the Western culture had taken notice of Japan's success and started to set and adhere to higher TQM guidelines, with an emphasis on "companywide quality," as opposed to just quality in manufacturing.

Also, during this time, Philip Crosby released his first book *Quality Is Free*. He made popular the concepts, "cost of quality," "zero defects," and "do it right the first time."

Around this time, TQM changed the game. TQM was a big shift from inspectors at the end of the production line inspecting finished products for defects. TQM essentially made the case, from the lessons of the previously mentioned quality gurus, that quality is a companywide

---

[5] Alansohn, et al. (2012).

responsibility. It is not the sole responsibility of the quality department to "find" defects.

Early in my career as a quality engineer, I worked at StorageTek, a large data storage company in Louisville, Colorado. In the late 1980s and early 1990s, StorageTek started their TQM journey. They called this effort Excellence Through Quality (ETQ)[6] and it was a companywide effort. There was plenty of messaging, planning, and training across all divisions and at all levels of management. As part of the quality organization, I was fortunate enough to be part of the early training sessions, then be involved with the implementation across different product lines, and eventually became part of the team that taught the training. Over the five years while focused on ETQ, revenues improved by 38 percent, revenue per employee went up by 27 percent, and external cost of quality went down from 31 percent to 5 percent. Additionally, StorageTek launched three of their most successful products, including their first automated tape library, their high availability disk array (known as Iceberg), and their virtual storage manager (VSM). The practices and methods taught through ETQ helped made that possible.

TQM provided a good framework for continuous improvement in the late 1980s and early 1990s. But companywide improvement efforts began to fizzle out, due in large part to a fading commitment from the top management.

Organizations such as the International Organization for Standardization (known as ISO) developed standards to further refine and provide a framework for consistent quality management systems. This includes the ISO 9000 Quality Management family of standards. But these are more about structure and consistency than improvement.

More recently, methodologies such as Six Sigma and Lean concepts have become more popular. Six Sigma and Lean concepts can drive significant improvements, although they do not have the same holistic view as did TQM.

Another change in recent years is the function now called QA (quality assurance). During the TQM era, QA meant assurance of quality for all

---

[6] Stratton (1994).

aspects of quality for a product. Today, QA is most often seen in product-based companies (hardware and software). In these companies, QA is essentially a test function. This is reminiscent of the pre-TQM days where inspectors were stationed at the end of the production line to check the product/assembly for defects. During the TQM days, most companies moved away from "inspecting the quality in" and held those that built the product responsible for building it correctly. The original TQM quality initiative that drove quality responsibilities across all functional groups is slowly disappearing. Today, many companies only have a QA team that is testing for defects. I realize test is an important function and we will discuss this in more detail in a later chapter. But here are my issues with this mindset. First, if you are using QA (i.e., test) as your *only* quality function, it is like beefing up one link in your chain instead of beefing up the whole chain. Second, by having QA be responsible for quality, you are letting the developers off the hook. *Preventing* defects is much more effective and productive than *searching* for them. For quality to have the type of impact described in the opening paragraph, these types of improvements must be made companywide, across all the functions.

A Note on Quality as It Pertains to Inspection and Test

For new products or new processes, you may need to set up some level of inspection and test to help ensure defects are caught before going on the next station or going to customers. But for any type of appraisal function (inspection or test), you should always consider it as a *temporary screen.* Your ultimate goal should be to eventually do away with that function. You do that by measuring the process, analyzing (to root cause) all the defects found at that step, and fixing them. You continue to measure, analyze, and fix until the process is so robust you no longer need to inspect or test.

There are many notable contributors to the discipline of quality, with each making their own impact toward the improvement of businesses. But three of the most well-known quality gurus are Juran, Deming, and Crosby. Below is a brief background of these notable quality experts.

Juran[7]

Joseph Juran was an engineer and a management consultant. After World War II, Juran became a professor of industrial engineering at New York University, teaching quality control. Dr. Juran's work in the field of quality management drew interest in Japan, and in 1954 he went there to discuss his theories at the invitation of the Japanese Union of Scientists and Engineers. He continued teaching his quality management techniques, which became firmly embedded in the Japan's engineering and manufacturing industries. In 1979, Juran founded the Juran Institute. He published several books, most notably the *Quality Control Handbook*.

The Juran Trilogy

1. *Quality Planning.* Quality planning refers to the process of preparing to achieve quality. Planning is done to meet objectives. Clear objectives are needed before starting the plan. Quality planning is the activity of developing the products and processes required to meet customer's needs.

2. *Quality Control.* Quality control consists of evaluating the actual quality performance, comparing it the actual performance to quality goals, and acting on the difference.

3. *Quality Improvement.* This process is the means of raising quality performance to new levels ("breakthrough"). His methodology consists of a series of structured steps.

Deming[8]

W. Edwards Deming was a business consultant and statistician. He and Juran are considered the fathers of the modern quality movement. After World War II, he was invited to work in Japan, where he greatly influenced Japanese industry, specifically in Statistical Process Control (SPC)

---

[7] Juran (1951).

[8] Gitlow and Gitlow (1987).

and Total Quality Management (TQM). In 1982, he published his book *Out of the Crisis*. In this book, he published his 14 points for delivering quality products.

The 14 Points

1. *Create a constant purpose toward improvement.* This is building a plan for quality in the long term and resist reacting with short-term solutions. Don't settle for doing the same things better—find better things to do.
2. *Adopt the new philosophy.* This speaks to sharing the responsibility for quality throughout the organization. Create your quality vision and implement it.
3. *Stop depending on inspections.* You can't inspect quality into a product (same goes for test). Inspections are costly and unreliable—and they don't improve quality, they merely find a lack of quality. Build quality into the process from start to finish.
4. *Use a single supplier for any one item.* Deming believed that quality relies on consistency—the less variation you have in the input, the less variation you'll have in the output. Look at suppliers as your partners in quality.
5. *Improve constantly and forever.* Continuously improve your systems and processes. Deming promoted the Plan-Do-Check-Act approach to process analysis and improvement.
6. *Use training on the job.* Train for consistency to help reduce variation. Build a foundation of common knowledge. Encourage employees to learn from one another and provide a culture and environment for effective teamwork.
7. *Implement leadership.* Expect your management team to understand their workers and the processes they use. Don't just supervise—provide the support and resources needed so each employee can do his or her best.
8. *Eliminate fear.* Allow people to perform at their best by creating an environment where they're not afraid to express ideas or concerns. Ensure that your leaders are approachable and that they work with

teams to act in the company's best interests. Use open and honest communication to remove fear from the organization.

9. *Break down barriers between departments.* Create a shared vision and use cross-functional teamwork to build understanding and reduce confrontational relationships. Focus on collaboration instead of compromise.

10. *Get rid of unclear slogans.* Let people know exactly what you want—don't make them guess.

11. *Eliminate management by objectives.* Eliminate quotas and targets and understand how the process is carried out. Deming said that production targets encourage high output and low quality. Measure the process rather than the people behind the process.

12. *Remove barriers to pride of workmanship.* This again points to the importance of culture. Allow everyone to take pride in their work without being rated or compared.

13. *Implement education and self-improvement.* Encourage people to learn new skills to prepare for future changes and challenges. Build skills to make your workforce more adaptable to change, and better able to find and achieve improvements.

14. *Make "transformation" everyone's job.* It takes buy-in from everyone to make a transformation. Again, this talks to a shared vision to everyone can relate to and everyone understands their part in making the change.

Crosby[9]

Philip Crosby was a leading quality professional, consultant, and author. He is widely recognized for promoting the concept of "zero defects" and "cost of quality." In 1979, he founded Philip Crosby Associates, Inc. (PCA), teaching management how to establish a preventive culture to get things done right the first time. Crosby's first book, *Quality Is Free*, was credited with playing a large part in beginning the quality revolution in the United States and Europe. In this book, he listed his 14 steps to improvement.

---

[9] Crosby (1979).

The 14 Steps to Quality Improvement

Step 1—Management Commitment. For change to happen, there needs to be commitment from the top that is communicated across the organization. Crosby said, "Do not confuse 'communication' with 'motivation.' The results of communication are real and long-lasting; the results of motivation are shallow and short-lived."

Step 2—Quality Improvement Team. Bring together representatives of each department to form the quality improvement team. These should be people who can speak for their departments to commit operations to actions.

Step 3—Quality Measurement. Quality measurements for each area of activity must be established where they don't exist and reviewed where they do. Formalizing the company measurement system strengthens the other functions and ensures proper measurement.

Step 4—Cost of Quality Evaluation. Initial measurement estimates are likely to be shaky (although low), and so it is necessary at this point to get more accurate figures. Cost of quality (COQ) is not an absolute performance measurement; it is an indication of where corrective action will be profitable for a company. Much more on COQ in later chapters.

Step 5—Quality Awareness. This is the step where you show employees the data of what "non-quality" is costing. This is an important step in that it puts a number (even if it's an estimate) on what lack of quality can cost a company. By using cost of quality as the measurement, you prioritize your efforts by where it's costing you the most.

Step 6—Corrective Action. As quality awareness grows and employees pay attention to the costs associated with non-quality, or the cost of poor quality (COPQ), the opportunities for effective corrective action will become more and more evident. This will start the habit of identifying and correcting problems.

Step 7—Establish an Ad Hoc Committee for the Zero Defects Program. Crosby made zero defects the standard for quality. He suggested you select three or four members of the improvement team to investigate the zero defects concept and ways to implement the program. Its purpose is to communicate to all employees the literal meaning of the words "zero defects" and the thought that everyone should do things right the first time.

Step 8—Supervisor Training. Conduct a formal orientation with all levels of management prior to implementation of all the steps. All managers must understand each step well enough to explain it to their people.

Step 9—Zero Defects Day. Establishment of zero defects as the performance standard of the company should be done in one day. That way, everyone understands it the same way.

Step 10—Goal Setting. During meetings with employees, each manager requests they establish the goals they would like to strive for. Usually, there should be 30-, 60-, and 90-day goals.

Step 11—Error Cause Removal. Ask individuals to describe any problem that keeps them from performing error free work on a simple, one-page form.

Step 12—Recognition. Establish award programs to recognize those who meet their goals or perform outstanding acts. Genuine recognition of performance is something people really appreciate.

Step 13—Quality Councils. Bring the quality professionals and team chairpersons together regularly to communicate with each other and determine actions necessary to upgrade and improve the solid quality program being installed.

Step 14—Do It Over Again. The typical program takes a year to eighteen months. By that time, turnover and changing situations will have wiped out most of the education effort. Therefore, it is necessary to set up a new team of representatives and begin again.

Guru Summary

The philosophies of Juran, Deming, and Crosby varied across topics from slightly different to complete disagreement. However, the areas where they were aligned across their improvement strategies were goals, measurement, culture, and training.

Goals. For any type of improvement, it is important to set a target. Where do you want to be? What do you want to accomplish?

Measurement. How do you know when you have reached your goals? You need to establish some type of measurement system to determine whether you are on track or if adjustments need to be made.

Culture. You cannot expect improvement to take place in a poor or toxic culture. Employees need to feel safe and motivated to do their best.

Training. Once your plan is in place, you will need consistent communication and teach everyone how to implement your system.

We will talk discuss each of these areas in more depth when we get to the new quality model.

CHAPTER 2

Quality Models and Methods

Overview of Common Quality Models

There have been many popular quality models and methodologies over the last several decades.[1] I have had to opportunity to work with each of these models, to varying degrees. So, below is a brief synopsis of some that are most familiar based on my experience with them.

ISO 9000

ISO 9000 is a series of international standards to help companies effectively document their quality management system (QMS). They are not specific to any one industry and the ISO 9000 certification verifies your company complies to the standard. There are many other standards, such as for medical devices and food. But the ISO 9000 set of standards are most broadly used. The common phrase given to keep the ISO implementation as reasonably simple as possible is: "Say what you do and do what you say." There are some companies and countries that will not accept a product if your business is not ISO certified.

Key Point. ISO certification conveys to customers that you have met a tangible standard that provides them confidence in your ability to produce a quality product or service.

---

[1] Alansohn, et al. (2012).

Quality Management System

A quality management system (QMS) defines the elements required within your business model for ISO compliance. These elements normally include customer focus, leadership, engagement of people, supplier quality, continuous improvement, document management, process management, and corrective and preventative action.

Key Point. A QMS provides a repeatable structure that helps you consistently meet your quality needs, as long as you maintain it. I have seen where a QMS was put in place to achieve ISO certification. Once certified, the QMS was never updated (at least until the next audit). If you are going to take the time to establish a QMS, make it useful and update it as your business changes.

Statistical Process Control

One of the best practices in quality is to identify defects as early as possible. Control of key processes so that issues can be detected early as possible and can be done through statistics. Statistical process control (SPC) is a set of methods first created by Walter A. Shewhart at Bell Laboratories in the early 1920s. W. Edwards Deming standardized SPC for the American industry during World War II and introduced it to Japan after the war. SPC quantitatively measures the outputs of a process, looking for small but statistically significant changes, so that corrections can be made quickly. SPC was first used within manufacturing, where it could help reduce waste from rework and scrap. However, SPC can be used for any process that has a measurable output. SPC is used to monitor processes through control charts to show whether a process is in control or not. Control limits are used to provide quick identification of points outside the expected variance of the process.

Key Point. SPC is an invaluable tool to measure and monitor your processes. When used properly, SPC gives you an "early alert" system to head off major problems.

Total Quality Management

Some background on total quality management (TQM) was provided earlier. With TQM, everyone in the company or organization is responsible for quality assurance and problem prevention. TQM uses business strategy, data analysis, and communication across different business functions to improve quality across the company and the processes of the organization. Many of the TQM concepts are exceptionally good, starting with the idea that quality is a companywide effort. However, the larger the company, the larger the effort is to get everyone trained, coordinated, and committed. It requires strong leadership to keep the momentum going.

Key Point. TQM is a companywide approach to quality. I still believe there are some powerful concepts within TQM. In particular, there is great value in everyone working together toward a common goal.

Lean

Lean began from a manufacturing process that was developed by Toyota in 1988, known as the Toyota production system (TPS). It is based upon two key principles: the removal of irregularity and the removal of irrelevance. Specifically, this means trying to get uniformity within production and removing wasteful steps or processes. The main idea behind a Lean process is to get the most efficient process within a production environment. Lean strives to create the most consistently good product in the most efficient way. However, Lean is not limited to a production environment. Lean principles are now being used across a variety of industries, such as health care, hospitality, and government agencies.

Key Point. Lean principles focus on removing waste and improving productivity. Lean provides a continuous emphasis on seeking out and eliminating waste. This helps you to reduce costs and improve value.

Six Sigma

Six Sigma is a methodology focused on creating breakthrough improvements by managing variation and reducing defects in processes across the enterprise. If we can measure the process variations that cause defects, that is, unacceptable deviation from the mean or target, we can work toward systematically managing the variation to eliminate defects. Introduced at Motorola in the mid-1980s, Six Sigma was initially targeted to quantify the defects occurring during manufacturing processes, and to reduce those defects to a very small level. Motorola claimed to have saved several million dollars. GE also experienced popular success. Six Sigma contributed over $300 million to GE's 1997 operating income. The Six Sigma belt system uses a ranking structure similar to the belt structure used in martial arts disciplines to identify levels of expertise in the Six Sigma methods.

Key Point. Six Sigma provides quantitative tools and a structured approach to drive improvement on a specific project. Six Sigma is more tactical compared to TQM, which is more strategic.

While all the above methodologies have been successful, why has there not been one dominate methodology? Why do some efforts fizzle out? What is missing or why have they not been sustainable?

I believe the missing ingredient is *culture*. Without a strong and healthy culture, none of these methodologies will work for the long term. How can you focus on improvement for the long term when there is fear, doubt, or confusion in the organization? You need a solid foundation to implement change. We will be taking a much deeper dive into culture and how it relates to quality in the following chapter.

CHAPTER 3

The New Model

The Sustainable Quality Model

I believe there is a new holistic way to look at quality. It starts by building a strong foundation. You need a solid foundation as your base to build and grow your quality strategy. I believe that foundation should be a culture of quality. You need to develop a culture that truly embraces what you are trying to build. On top of that foundation, you need to create vision. You need a roadmap to show where you are going, with clear goals and objectives to get you there. You cannot expect anyone to follow you if they do not know where you are going. Once you have a direction, you need to provide the tools and the training to accomplish the goals and objectives. The new model is shown in Figure 3.1.

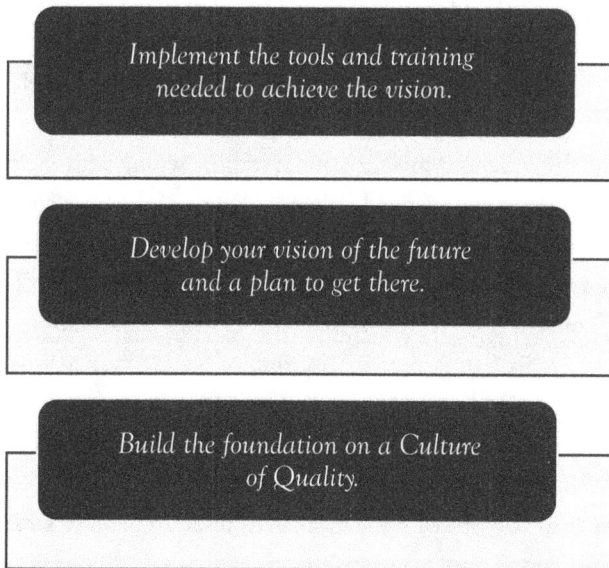

Implement the tools and training needed to achieve the vision.

Develop your vision of the future and a plan to get there.

Build the foundation on a Culture of Quality.

Figure 3.1a

Figure 3.1b New quality model

A New Approach

I believe that where most improvement efforts fail is that culture is either not ready to embrace the initial change, not ready to sustain the changes after they are made, or both. Even the best methods and tools will fall short if they are introduced into an environment that is not ready for them. This can happen when top management pushes a methodology from the top and the culture does not embrace it. I have been in companies where I experienced this firsthand. Nothing wrong with the methodology, but the change never had a chance. At one of the large companies I worked at, one of the executives heard from his peers at other technology companies that Six Sigma helped them with some significant improvements. Soon after, there was a mandate that all organizations needed to complete a Six Sigma project. A group of Six Sigma black belts were brought in to assist the organizations. The culture was never prepared for this type of mandate. I remember talking with other managers and the general feeling was this is another program of the month. A few of us managers tried to work with the black belts to do something meaningful. But by and large, most managers just went through the motions to get this checked off their "to do" list.

In these situations, it is not unusual for people to just go through the motions. At best, it will fizzle out as soon as top management loses interest or moves the priority to something else. The worst case is trying to introduce change into a dysfunctional or even toxic environment. It is a waste of everyone's time. Most people in those types of environments are either looking to survive or looking to leave. In this type of culture, people are not likely to go "above and beyond." In a toxic culture, it is more likely "I'm doing the bare minimum, until I can find a way out of this situation." They most certainly are not focused on process improvement. Fix the culture before you can fix the process.

I worked at a small tech startup that had a stressful and demanding environment. We talked about improvements, but they were never a priority until there was an issue. Frustration and burnout turned into people leaving. It was not the average or above average performers that got frustrated and left the company first. It was the top performers that could walk out the door and immediately find a new job.

A *long-term, sustained* commitment to quality only comes from employees that feel good about what they are doing and feel good about who they work for. This type of dedication is often referred to as a "culture of quality" and only comes from a work environment and leadership that values each employee. This type of culture creates a sense of belonging and pride in the company, as well as its products/services. To develop this type of culture you must drive out fear, break down barriers, and provide employees with the vision, tools and support that "inspires" them to do their best. This culture is fundamental to any *sustainable* change.

What Is Culture?

When we talk about culture, what exactly do we mean? Culture represents the beliefs, values, rules of behavior, attitudes, and norms that reflect a company's values and modes of operation. It is the day-to-day environment that everyone works within. Every company has a culture—but not all cultures are conducive to helping a company achieve its goals. It is not unusual for companies to have a "stated culture," and another that is the "real culture." The "stated culture" may sound good on paper or on a website but may not be true.

Some of the main components that make up a culture might include:

- Behaviors based on people interactions.
- Norms for how employees work together, individually and in groups.
- Dominant values adopted by the organization.
- Rules of the game for getting ahead.
- The overall climate.

Additionally, there are key factors that influence a culture that should be considered:

Business Environment

- Social values
- Diversity
- Company maturity
- Outside influences
- Competition

Type of Company

- Industry
- Products/technology
- Size
- History
- Market position
- Quality maturity

Employees

- Values
- Attitudes
- Knowledge
- Experience
- Collaboration
- Loyalty/commitment

Leadership

- Vision
- Management style
- Communication style
- Growth opportunities
- Pay structures
- Benefits
- Recognition
- Teamwork
- Work conditions

Warning Signs

It may not always be easy to spot a problematic culture. Especially, if you are not looking for it. Culture can exist on multiple levels. The working environment at the top levels is not necessarily the same as at the lower levels. Problems occurring at the worker level may not be seen at the executive level, depending on the size of the company. To create real and lasting change, your business must tackle cultural issues on all levels. Changing your culture is a challenging process, but it is not impossible. With the right approach, you can turn around the mindset of your employees. It starts with understanding some of the warning signs. Do you recognize any of these warning signs in your workplace?

- *Missed Deadlines.* Consistently (or too frequently) missing key deadlines. There can be several causes, but it is important to understand why commitments are not being met. Are the deadlines realistic? Were the people doing the work involved in setting the deadline? Was their input ignored? Have they been properly trained?
- *Mistakes/Errors/Defects.* Consistently finding mistakes or errors that need to be resolved. This would include finding new errors or repeated errors. Consistently dealing with issues is time-consuming and costly. It is important to know that human errors are consequences, not causes. To understand the

root cause of these errors, deeper analysis is needed. Do not accept that the root cause for the mistakes was due to human error. If humans are making mistakes, there is a reason. Do not treat the symptom; get to the actual root cause.

- *Inefficiencies.* It is possible that work is getting done. But it takes too long, or it requires additional work to make it right. This can also be where certain work items are not always done the same way, leading to greater variation in the results.

- *Customer Complaints.* Nothing can derail a company faster than unhappy customers. Typically, less than 5 percent of unhappy customers will complain directly to you. On average, a dissatisfied customer will tell 10 or more people about their poor experience. In many cases, it takes 40 positive customer experiences to make up for a single bad experience.

- *Turnover/Absenteeism.* Losing good talent and experience can be costly for any company, especially when there is little overlap or cross-training in place. The cost to bring a new employee up to speed is expensive (in time and money). Employee turnover has a direct impact on company revenue and profitability. The cost of replacing an employee can be 50–100 percent of their annual salary, depending on position. These costs include advertising, interviewing, screening, and hiring. Then it may take a new employee one to two years to reach the productivity of the previous person, which might directly impact your customers. This also has an impact on remaining employees who see the high turnover and become more disengaged and less productive.

- *Team Dysfunction.* While some amount of disagreement or difference of opinion is healthy, too much can become a problem. Also watch for lack of team communication or collaboration. The dysfunction could be horizontal (across groups) or vertical (manager to employee).

- *Impact on Quality.* It is easy to see how these types of issues can have a negative impact on quality. You want to be at your best to produce your best. But if you are hampered by mistakes, turnover, and dysfunction, you are certainly not at your best. You need to understand the root cause for these issues before you can focus on improving. For most, if not all, of these issues, the cause may be directly tied to your culture. Culture can make or break an improvement effort as well as the company. We will be focus more closely on the relationship between culture and quality in the next section.

Tier I: Quality Culture

What Is a Quality Culture?

A long-term, *sustained* commitment to quality only comes from employees that feel good about what they are doing. This means a sense of purpose and a role that contributes to that purpose. They need to feel good about who they work for. At a micro level, this means their direct boss. Do they trust her or him? At a macro level, this is the company. Do they believe in top leadership and the direction they have the company headed? When these all align and the employee feels safe, confident, and motivated, they become dedicated. This type of dedication is often referred to as a "culture of quality." It only comes from a productive work environment, where employees feel valued and appreciated. This type of culture creates a sense of belonging and pride in the company and its products/services. To develop this type of culture, you must drive out fear, break down barriers, and provide employees with the vision, tools and support that "inspires" them to do their best. *A quality culture is fundamental to any sustained change.*

Think of a time in your personal or work life, where you were genuinely inspired and entirely focused on doing your absolute best on some project, task, or job. How did you feel about the environment you were working in? Was it safe? Supportive? Even encouraging? How did you feel about the actual work you were doing? Confident? Challenged? Maybe a stretch for you from previous work? Think about the driving factors that made this important to you? Was there a sense of achievement? A sense of pride? Were you a part of a team that you could not let down? Were you breaking new ground on something that had not been done before within your circle of friends, your family, or with coworkers?

If these questions help you conjure up that image of a special time in your life, when you were at your absolute best, then you know what an ideal quality culture is.

Now think about your current work environment. Is there a sense of pride that spans companywide? Is each person inspired to do their best? Or does the environment (culture) strip that inherent desire away from them? If it is the latter, can you honestly expect a continuous improvement effort to take hold?

Developing pride in your company is hard. But unfortunately, destroying pride in workmanship and the company is easy. Ignore a worker that raises a potential issue (or worse, chastise them for it), force them to work long hours (on a regular basis) or without the tools and training to be successful, demand results based on unclear or unreasonable expectations. All of these contribute to a poor culture. Additionally, you must eliminate any type of harassment from your workplace. This includes bullying and unprofessional behavior from anyone in a position of authority. All too often, top management does not see the middle manager or lead technical person that bullies or belittles other employees in meetings or hallways. Even worse, top management knows about it and looks the other way. This is unacceptable, no matter how much you depend on those technical skills.

Ask yourself if any of the symptoms we discussed earlier reflect your current environment: dysfunctional teams, increased employee turnover or absenteeism, customer complaints, increased mistakes, errors, defects, missed deadlines, lack of results, low productivity, increased product returns, and increasing costs.

Take a few minutes and do this little experiment. Go to a site, such as Glassdoor, that has ratings on the different companies. Randomly pick a few companies that have lower ratings. Now go look at the reviews of those lower rated companies. Do you see any comments similar to the common business warning signs or pain points we mentioned above? What do the comments say about the leadership of that business? How is your company rated and what comments do you see from current or previous employees?

You can either create your culture or you let it happen. As a leader, you must consciously create an environment that allows, encourages, and even inspires people to care and want to do their best. The famous management consultant and writer Peter Drucker[1] was credited with the quote, "Culture eats strategy for breakfast." It is not the strategy is unimportant. It is just that having a strong and healthy culture is required before any strategy has a chance to work. Beyond the focus on quality, *a healthy culture is essential for the success of your business.*

The well-known author and consultant Stephen Covey shared his thoughts on quality and culture. Covey[2] talks about an outside-in approach to quality, as compared to an inside-out approach. The outside-in approach is driven by outside influences, like management and "program of the month" scenarios. But the inside-out approach is internally motivated. As Covey states, you can hire the hands and backs of people, but they volunteer their minds and hearts. You get the most out of people when they work in an empowering environment and feel a sense of accomplishment.

Culture and Motivation

Culture shapes employee motivation. Understanding motivation (and de-motivation) may help you to develop a more desired work environment. Recall the Maslow Theory of Motivation.

- We each have a hierarchy of needs that range from "low" to "high."
- Maslow's theory maintains that a person does not reach for a higher need until the need of current level have been satisfied.
- Maslow's hierarchy pyramid[3] shows five levels.

Applying Maslow's hierarchy to the workplace:

1. Level 1—Physiological needs: Provide ample breaks and pay salaries that allow workers to buy life essentials.

---

[1] Hyken (2015).
[2] Covey (1994).
[3] Research History (2012).

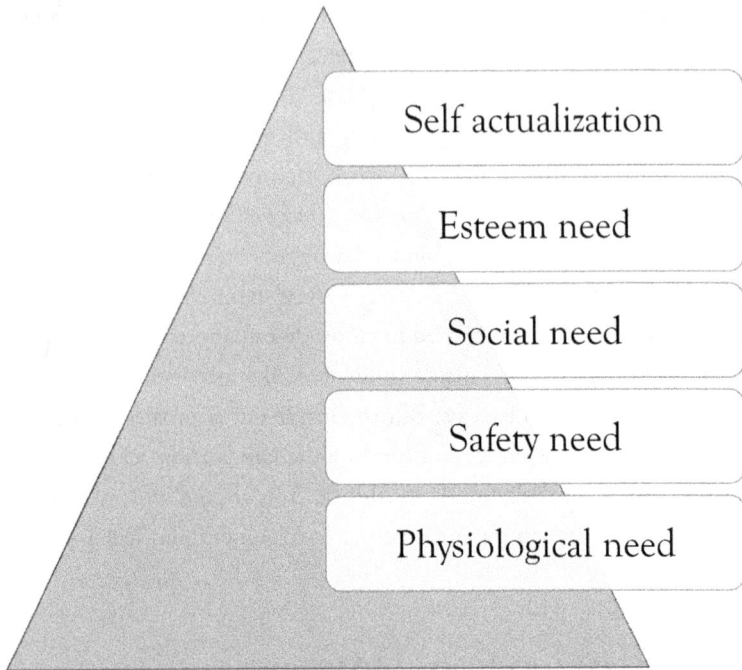

Figure 3.2 Maslow's hierarchy of needs

2. Level 2—Safety needs: Provide a safe environment for work, relative job security, and freedom from threats and harassment.
3. Level 3—Social needs: Generate a feeling of acceptance, belonging by reinforcing a team dynamic.
4. Level 4—Esteem needs: Recognize achievements, utilize talent appropriately, and provide status to make employees feel valued and appreciated.
5. Level 5—Self-actualization: Offer challenging and meaningful work assignments.

But how do these basic needs tie into quality? Table 3.1 shows how the levels align.

Now if we take this one step further, Table 3.2 looks at how we transition from a traditional company culture to a quality culture:

Table 3.1

Maslow's Hierarchy	Satisfies Maslow's Needs	Impact on Quality
Self-actualization Needs	Creative and challenging work Participation in decision making Job flexibility and autonomy	Cultural alignment, trust in policies, beliefs, methods, and communications within the company. Opportunities are clear and achievable.
Esteem needs	Responsibility for important job Promotion to higher status job Praise and recognition from boss	Organizational trust in company's products, direction, leaders and doing the right thing. You feel compelled to do things right.
Social needs	Friendly coworkers Interaction with customers Likable boss	Interpersonal trust with other coworkers and team members. Collaboration is the norm.
Safety needs	Safe working conditions Job security Base compensation and benefits	Managerial trust with your direct manager and overall leadership. You feel appreciated and supported.
Physiologic needs	Rest breaks Physical comfort on the job Reasonable work hours	Comfortable work environment and comfortable work conditions.

Table 3.2

Traditional Culture	Quality Culture
Hierarchical style	Participative style
Top-down information flow	Top-down, lateral, and upward information flow
Inward quality focus	Customer defined quality focus
Functional focus	Process focus
Short-term planning	A vision for the future
Sporadic improvements	Sustainable continuous improvement
Top-down initiatives	All staff involved and engaged
Manage and delegate	Lead and coach
Direct	Empower
Counsel	Ownership and participation
Functional and narrow scope on jobs	Integrated functions
Enforcement	Promoting mutual trust
Firefighting—a few individuals/groups	Team initiatives—focus on continuous improvement

Demotivators

We talked about how culture can shape motivation. But some management actions can quickly de-motivate employees, adversely affecting culture. Here are some of the more common demotivators:

1. When an employee hates their boss. Most employees quit their boss, not the company. If the employee cannot trust their direct boss, at the very least they will be demotivated. More likely they will eventually leave.

2. Having a toxic culture. A bad culture can suck the productivity out of people and kills any creativity. This is the top reason for high turnover.

3. Overwork your people. It is not unreasonable to occasionally expect some long hours from your employees. But if "occasionally" turns into "ongoing or normal," that is a problem. Demanding more and more from your employees leads to burnout, more mistakes, and higher absenteeism.

4. A lack of vision. Everyone looks for meaning in their jobs. They want to know they are contributing something that makes the work rewarding. Give them a reason for what they are doing, "a constancy of purpose," as Deming stated.

5. Unclear expectations and poor communication. It is hard to hit the target when you don't know what the target is. This can be so frustrating for an employee. You should never have to guess if you are working on the right thing or doing things right.

6. Harassment. Any type of harassment or bullying causes disengagement. These types of issues will continue to escalate until someone quits or gets fired.

7. Micromanaging. Overmanaging or babysitting employees that do not need it kills creativity and confidence. It either drives them to stop thinking or drives them to leave.

8. Lack of on-boarding plan. Nothing worse than bringing a new person on board and have nothing ready for them, such as a workspace, initial tasks, training, and so on. All the enthusiasm they came into the company with will begin to fade away quickly.

9. No consistency. Why establish processes, policies, and procedures if they are not enforced? It is especially bad when management continues to make exceptions or excuses for not following the very processes they wanted in place.
10. Not addressing poor performance or addressing it to the general workforce (instead confronting the poor performer directly). It is never comfortable to confront an employee on a performance issue. However, that is part of manager's responsibility and it impacts others when they see that poor performance is not addressed. It is no help to the poor performer either, if they do not realize there is a problem. Hold your employees accountable but do so by getting to the root of the problem (e.g., Are the requirements clear? Is there a training issue?) You need to understand the problem before you can address it.
11. Treating everyone equally (when the performance is not equal). This is the opposite of number 10. This is giving everyone credit when the workload is not balanced. You need to understand who is contributing and who is not. Assuming everything is equal when it is not can be very demotivating for the person or persons carrying the load.
12. Management not following through on their promises. If your employees cannot trust you, they will not follow you. Do what you say you will.

Tier II: Quality Strategy

If we look at the next level in the sustainable quality model, the middle tier is a quality strategy.

We can break the strategy into three key parts:

1. *Shared vision* (future state). This is where you create your lofty shared view of the future.
2. *Current realty* (current state). It is important to know where you currently are, so you can assess that gap to the future. Be honest with yourself.
3. *Action plan* (the gap). The gap is about building that bridge. It is your plan of action. The details of your action plan get worked out through goals and metrics.

Figure 3.3 shows how these three parts all fit together.

Your quality strategy should have a positive influence on your culture. It feeds into the social, esteem, and self-actualization needs discussed previously. Having a clearly stated direction is empowering. Team interactions will improve and day-to-day decision-making gets better. This is possible when you have a well communicated strategy and vision. Every decision should be determined based on whether it helps or hinders you from reaching your immediate goals and ultimately your vision.

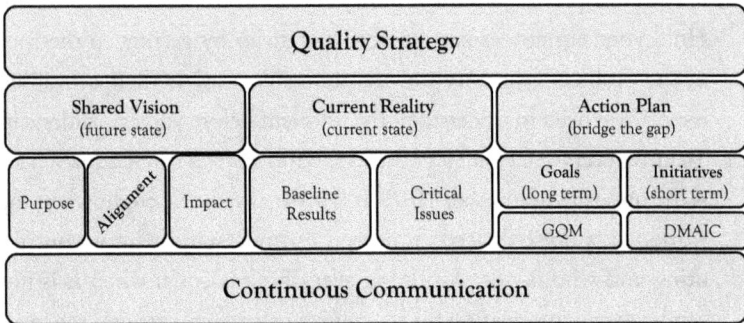

Figure 3.3 Quality strategy model

Shared Vision

Every business should have a clear and well-articulated vision of their future. Having a clear picture of where you want to be is a critical success factor. You often hear of elite athletes that use visualization as a key part of their training. It is equally, if not more important in business. A clear vision should provide hope, purpose, and inspiration. When we talk about vision for sustainable quality, it is not referring to the company vision statement. However, the quality vision should support the corporate vision. The important point is that building a quality strategy also starts with a vision. With respect to quality, where do you want to be in one year? three years? five years?

I have found that vision can be a polarizing word. You have people, like me, that get excited when I hear the word vision. I get excited because it immediately makes me think about possibilities, opportunities, and getting better. In fact, significantly better. But for others, vision is instantly associated with "change" or "dreaming." Not everyone embraces change. Some people are unsure about working toward something that is not tangible or demonstrable. This should not stop you from creating your new vision. Just be aware of the challenges and that some people will be much harder to convince than others.

The vision for quality, and for the entire business, should be a well-defined and set a clear image of the future. And not just a vision, but a "shared vision." Peter Senge,[4] in his book *The Fifth Discipline* says, at its simplest level, a shared vision is the answer to the question, "What do we want to create?" "It's not an organizational mandate." "When people truly share a vision they are connected, bound together by a common aspiration." Your work becomes part of something larger. There is a sense of purpose. If you have the right culture, a shared vision can be a powerful thing, pulling everyone together to accomplish something remarkable.

From a quality perspective, your vision should paint an inspiring picture of your future state. It needs to be defined clearly, in measurable terms. If you cannot clearly define it, how will you know if you get there? That is not to say that things cannot change along the way (and they most likely will), in which you will have to adjust. But the more specific you are, the better you can put a plan in place to get you there.

Think about what is important to your business. This might include:

- Improving customer satisfaction
- Reducing time to market
- Improving margins
- Reducing operational costs
- Reducing rework, repair, retest, scrap

A shared vision is about creating excitement and passion. It should inspire action and propel you into improving your customer's experience, your employee's experience, and your overall business success.

When Fusion-io got acquired by SanDisk, we had a small but highly talented quality and reliability team. After the acquisition, we got moved

---

[4] Senge (1990).

into the SanDisk Corporate Quality group but continued to support the Fusion-io manufacturing and engineering teams, which also got moved into corporate groups. As the postacquisition planning and integration continued, it became evident our group would eventually be split up or laid off. However, there were a few things we learned during that integration period. We were much more advanced in our tracking of field performance, as well as our overall quality reporting including the work we were doing with cost of quality. Additionally, we knew we had strong supporters for these functions in the manufacturing and engineering ranks. So, in an attempt to save jobs, I proposed we reinvent ourselves and create a center of excellence. We had some long team meetings to flush out this new vision. We put together a final proposal that emphasized these focus areas and how we could help other groups. I called on some business leaders to voice their support for our work and I pitched the proposal to the head of corporate quality. He bought in completely. The vision to do something bigger and better completely revitalized my team, as we went from thinking our jobs were at risk to working across the entire company, raising the bar for all product lines.

Current Reality

Before you get to where you want to be, you must know where you are starting from. If you have measurements in place already, you are a step ahead. If not, you will need to create a baseline as your starting point.

1. Establish a baseline. This is an important step to understand the climb toward your future state.
   (a) Where are you at today?
   (b) What's working?
   (c) What's not working?
   (d) Why is it not working?
   (e) What measurements are in place?
   (f) What *can* be measured, that is *not*?
      ○ Defect rates?
      ○ Cost?
      ○ Cycle time?

Start collecting and analyzing the data that you have.

Action Plan

Once you know your current state and where you wish to be. The "distance" between these two points is the very gap you need to bridge to succeed. This is where it takes some analysis to figure out the root causes for this gap.

Ask yourself the following questions:

- What actions and decisions caused our current position?
- Why did the gap happen?
- What could be done differently?
- What resources are required to achieve our goals?
- What are the critical issues we are dealing with today?
- What critical issues do we see in the foreseeable future?
- What changes/improvements can we make to incrementally get us to our desired (vision) state?

Goals (Long Term)

After you have assessed how far you are away from your future state, you should have some sense of the time it will take you to get there. You will have to consider all the factors that contribute to that timing (e.g., resources, budget, training, workloads, etc.). Achieving a lofty vision does happen overnight. So, chances are you are going to need some long-range goals (e.g., one year, five years, longer?). When planning long-term goals, you want them to be meaningful, clearly stated, and measurable. For these types of goals, I use a methodology called GQM.

GQM

Goals–questions–methods (GQM)[5] is a method or approach that was developed by Victor Basili and David Weiss when trying to find a better way to collect valid and useful data, while working on the NASA God-

---

[5] Basili (1992).

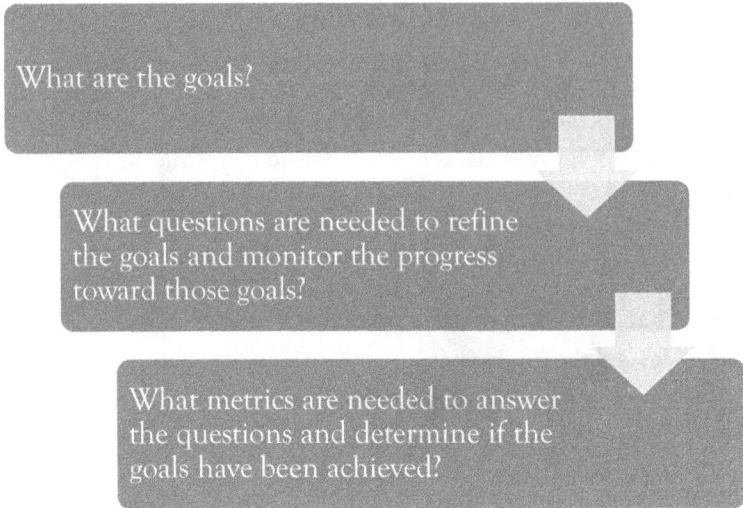

What are the goals?

What questions are needed to refine the goals and monitor the progress toward those goals?

What metrics are needed to answer the questions and determine if the goals have been achieved?

Figure 3.4 GQM flow

dard Space Flight Center. This is a top-down method, shown in Figure 3.4, that starts by creating a meaningful set of goals that you have set for your organization. You then develop the questions you want answered to help achieve those goals. Lastly, you define metrics that will help you answer those questions.

As you flush out the information about your goals, questions, and metrics, everything should tie back to your vision in the form of a tree structure.

Goals should tie back to the vision, questions should tie back to a goal, and metrics should tie back (and help answer) the questions.

There are probably more elaborate methods for developing and tracking GQM, depending on the scope and size of your effort. But for projects I have worked on, a simple spreadsheet has worked fine for documenting and tracking progress. Table 3.3 shows an example related to a new product validation effort and product readiness.

Addressing the Gap

Once you have your goals, questions, and metrics defined, you need to compare the current state to the future state. Where are you today

Table 3.3

Goals	Possible Questions	Possible Metrics
1. Provide a technical assessment of the risk associated with the validation of product requirements	a. Are the requirements clearly defined?	Approved requirements plan
	b. Are the requirements clearly understood and agreed to?	# of requirements validated
	c. Are the high-priority requirements identified?	# of requirements not tested
	d. What percentage of the requirements have been validated?	# of requirements failed
	e. What are the known risks (i.e., failures)?	# of requirement changes
	f. What are the unknown risks (i.e., untested requirements)?	
2. Communicate the status of customer relevant data, measuring "plan" versus "actual."	a. Does the product demonstrate required functionality?	# of open problems
	b. Does the product meet its expected Reliability, Availability, Serviceability goals?	# test cases planned/ executed
	c. Does the product meet its required agency standards?	# of hard failures
	d. Does the product meet its expected performance goals?	Mean Time Between Failures (MTBF) / Mean Time Between Interruptions (MTBI)
	e. Are the potential risks to our customers?	Fault detection/isolation %
	f. What are the impact of those risks?	Defects/1,000 hours of test
3. Maximize the cost effectiveness of the project by using the resources efficiently to drive defect detection earlier in the development process	a. What are the test escapes?	# of escapes
	b. What is the cost of the test effort, in:	People-hours

Table 3.3 (Continued)

Goals	Possible Questions	Possible Metrics
	* People/time?	In-house equipment costs
	* Equipment under test?	Infrastructure costs
	* Test infrastructure?	# of changes
	c. How many "restarts" due to product/code turns?	Average time to close problems
	d. How long do problems stay open?	tester time utilization
	e. How many problems had the "root cause" identified?	time to closure
4. Maximize the cost effectiveness of the project by using	a. What are the test escapes?	# of escapes

compared to the key goals you defined? What are the challenges or barriers preventing you from achieving those goals? What changes or improvements are needed to break through those barriers? Depending on how big the gap is, it may seem overwhelming. If it does, you need to break your action plan into reasonable deliverables. For the more short-term deliverables, which should tie to your longer-term goals, you can create a set of initiatives that can be accomplished using the Six Sigma DMAIC methodology. Select one of the goals and create a Six Sigma project to address it.

Six Sigma[6]

Every Six Sigma project uses a structured approach known as DMAIC. This acronym us made up from the first letters of each stage of the approach: define, measure, analyze, improve, and control. An overview of the methodology is shown in Figure 3.4.

Depending on the scope and size of your effort, your overall plan may look something like Figure 3.11.

---

[6] Alansohn, et al. (2012).

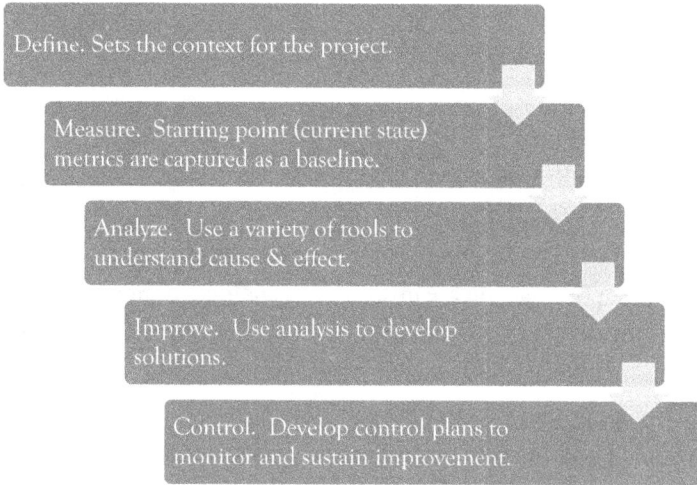

Define. Sets the context for the project.

Measure. Starting point (current state) metrics are captured as a baseline.

Analyze. Use a variety of tools to understand cause & effect.

Improve. Use analysis to develop solutions.

Control. Develop control plans to monitor and sustain improvement.

Figure 3.5 DMAIC methodology

Table 3.4 shows some of the key activities associated with each stage.

Table 3.4

Stage	Description	Key Activities
Define	Define the problem, goals, objectives	Develop a project charter, to include: project purpose, alignment of goals to vision, team members.
Measure	Establish a baseline	Develop detailed process maps, collect data from current process(es).
Analyze	Analyze the process and process data to understand the issue(s)	Analyze data, identify anomalies, and poor performance, develop root cause(s).
Improve	Develop solution(s) based on previous analysis	Identify possible solutions, rank/prioritize solutions, pilot top solutions.
Control	Develop a control plan to monitor and optimize the improvement(s)	Verify improvement, develop a control plan to monitor, close out project charter.

As we get into the next section, we will discuss in more detail, some of the specific tools that can help with the analyze phase and for closing the gap between the current state and the future state.

Tier III: Tools, Methods, and Training

At this point, you are developing a quality culture and have established a clear direction, with well-defined goals and action plans. You now need to equip your team with the resources they need to be successful. These resources would be the right tools, methods, and training to make them successful.

Cost of Quality

Introduction

As mentioned at the beginning of the book, cost of quality (COQ) is a measurement of what you are investing in good quality and what you are spending on poor quality. The best method for understanding how much poor quality is costing you, or conversely how much good quality can save you, is by using real dollars as the measurement.

Formalization of cost of quality was developed out of the work of Joseph Juran, Armand Feigenbaum, and Harold Freeman. The American Society for Quality's (ASQ) Quality Cost Committee worked to further formalize the concept and to promote its use. Phil Crosby's publication of *Quality Is Free*[7] provided probably the biggest boost to popularizing the COQ concept beyond the quality profession.

COQ is generally known as the sum of costs incurred to *prevent* nonconformances from happening (cost of conformance) and the costs incurred when nonconformance in products *do occur* (cost of nonconformance or "poor quality").

In companies that do not measure COQ, it is not uncommon for poor quality costs (nonconformance costs) to reach as high as 30 percent

Total Cost of Quality = Nonconformance Costs + Conformance Costs

of sales or more. As stated in the opening paragraph, that means you could be spending 1½ days each week, re-doing work that was not done right the first time. Stop and think about that, just for a minute. What additional work could be realized if you had that entire 1½ days back to work on new things?

Using COQ as the metric, you can plan improvement actions to prevent these poor quality problems and reduce the total COQ significantly. Because COQ is measured in dollars, the savings will ultimately boost the bottom line of the organization.

---

[7] Crosby (1979).

Putting a COQ program in place is not trivial. Most companies do not have a structure in place that easily allows tracking costs this way. But before we discuss an approach, it is important to understand the different COQ categories.

Cost of Quality Classifications

There are four types of costs captured into the total COQ, shown in Figure 3.6.

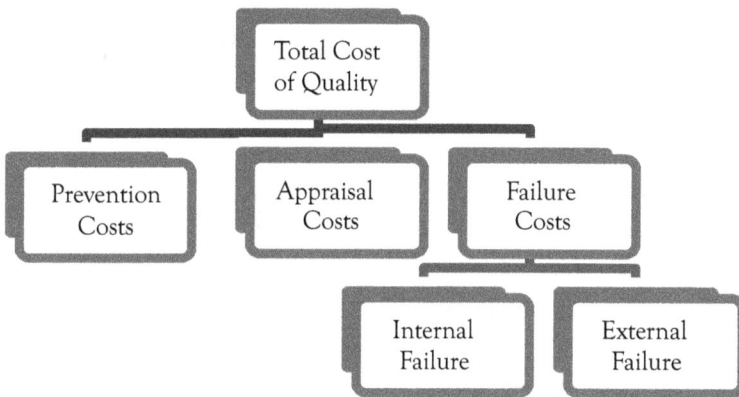

Figure 3.6 Cost of quality model

Prevention Costs

These are the costs associated with prevention of defects. This means identifying issues before the product is built or developed.

Examples:

- Formal design reviews
- Training (on product or process)
- Process design
- Requirement specifications (voice of the customer)
- Product design specifications
- Software complexity analysis

Appraisal Costs

These are costs associated with appraisal: inspection, test, audits. These are the costs of "searching" for defects. These costs happen after the product is built or developed.

Examples:

- Inspection (first pass only)
- Product testing (first pass only)
- Process measurements
- Product measurements
- Audits

Internal Failure Costs

These are the costs associated with internal defects from inspection, test, or audit. These are the costs of "finding" defects. These costs occur before the product is sent to a customer.

Examples:

- Rework
- Scrap
- Re-inspection (after initial inspection)
- Retest (after initial test)
- Lost time due to debug and defect removal
- Development of bug fixes
- Schedule delays

External Failure Costs

These are the costs associated with customer defects/issues. These are the costs of your customer "finding" defects. These costs occur after the product is sent to a customer.

Examples:

- Lost sales
- Replacement costs
- Shipping & Logistics costs due to a quality issue
- Support costs
- Customer downtime & liability costs
- Lost time (including executive time spent on issue)
- Rework
- Scrap
- Re-inspection (after initial inspection)
- Retest (after initial test)

- Lost time due to debug and defect removal
- Development of bug fixes

Understanding Cost of Quality

Understanding what your poor quality is costing you is essential to your business. Consider the cost of a dissatisfied customer.

- An average business doesn't hear from 96 percent of unhappy customers.
- Of those who complain, 50–70 percent will do business again if the complaint is resolved. And 95 percent will return if resolved quickly.
- An average customer with a complaint tells 9 to 10 people, 13 percent tell more than 20 people.
- Those who have complained and had a resolution tell five people.

Having tracked the quality costs associated with external failures (customer found issues), we found by far the significant impact from poor quality, was lost sales. As hard as it is to gain a trusted customer, it is quite easy to lose one.

When you are collecting the information for quality costs, it is important that you consider all of the costs. Some costs are not so visible. Examples of hidden costs are shown in the bottom half of the iceberg in Figure 3.7. The better you can account for these hidden costs, the more accurate your total quality costs will be.

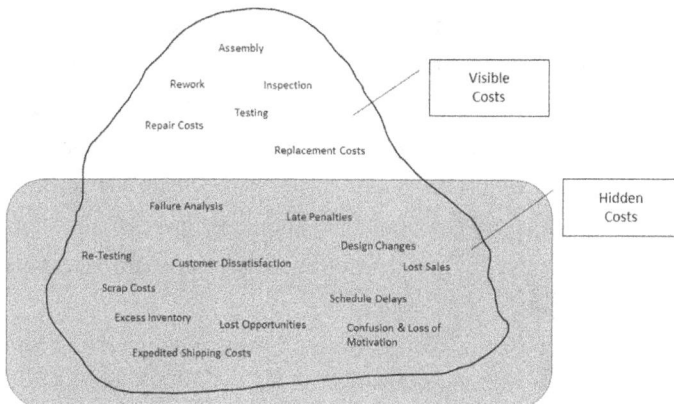

Figure 3.7 Hidden costs

Table 3.5 shows the *actual* quality costs associated with *one* product issue that impacted multiple customers. This resulted in a stop ship (i.e., all shipments put on hold until the issue was resolved) for that product.

Table 3.5

Cost Type	Amount
Man-hour costs (burdened)	$336,179
RMA/rework/logistics costs	$198,968
Opportunity and lost sales costs	$10,500,000
Total Stop Ship Costs	**$11,035,147**

If you add up all the costs associated with resolving this one issue, there are hard costs and soft costs. The hard costs included all the man-hours for all the people involved with resolving this issue. That includes the salespeople dealing directly with the customer, and it could involve executives getting on calls with the customer or even on a plane to meet the customer. It includes engineers working on failure analysis: root cause and then a fix. It involves test people testing the fix. It includes logistics people handling returned products. It also includes the hard costs of returned products and shipping out new products, which is often includes expedited fees in these situations. No doubt it is challenging to capture these man-hours and assign a pay rate to them. The logistics costs are a bit easier to track. But most difficult and most important are the soft costs that tell you the real impact. As you can see in the above example, these costs can be multiple orders of magnitude over the other costs. To gather the soft costs for this issue, I got on the phone and talked directly to the salesperson assigned to each of the top customers that experienced this particular issue. Some of those customers withdrew recently placed orders and some cancelled large orders they were about to place. Some customers stated they lost trust with us due to the issues and some stated that the delays impacted their timelines and they moved on to a competitor to fulfill their needs. The number above reflects all these lost orders. Again, this is for *one* specific issue.

Therefore, it is so important to focus on prevention instead of reacting to issues. Prevention has more leverage, so the priority should be "*prevention, not correction.*"

Putting a COQ program into place takes effort, training, and discipline. The biggest challenge comes in setting up the data collection needed to track all the costs. This is likely to be a manual effort to start. As with any new effort, the training is necessary to get a shared understanding of how COQ works and why it is important. Then the discipline is required to consistently collect and analyze the data. But once you have your process in place, it can be illuminating.

Trying to put the costs into the correct categories can be challenging at first. The flowchart in Figure 3.8 shows how to determine the correct cost category.

COQ DECISION FLOW

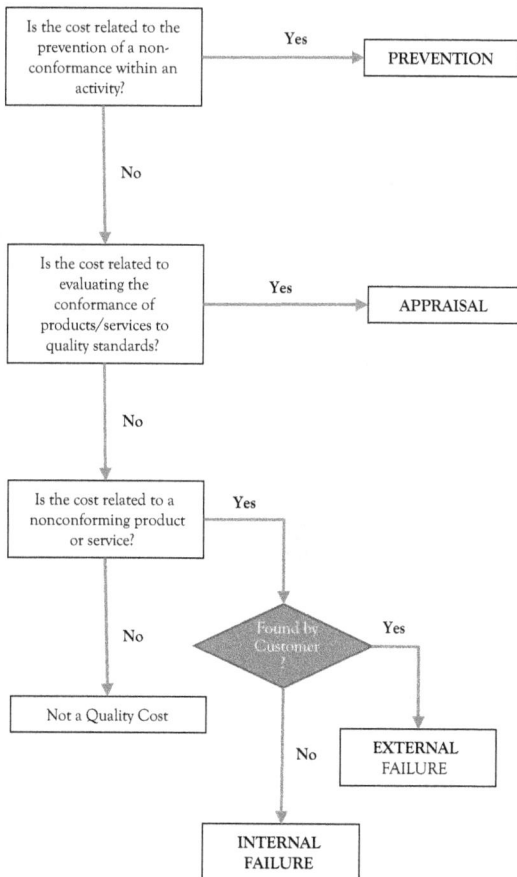

Figure 3.8 *Quality cost decisions*

Once the specific cost areas are determined for each cost category, a simple spreadsheet like the one in Figure 3.9 can be used to compile the data. In the next chapter, we will discuss some ways to make this easier in the "Quality for Finance" section.

Cost of Conformance	Man-Hours (avg burdened rate X total hrs)	Material (cost of parts/replacements)	Other Expenses (equip/depreciation, shipping, handling)
Prevention Costs			
Employee Training (as related to product or process)			
Design Reviews			
Quality Planning Activities			
Supplier Capability Surveys			
Preventative Maintenance on Development/Operations Equipment			
Process Capability Studies			
Quality Improvement Projects			
Statistical Process Control			
Early Prototyping			
Developing Fault-tolerant Designs			
Usability Analysis			
Developing Accurate Documentation			
Evaluating Tools (before buying them)			
Writing Clear/Accurate Specifications			
Requirements Analysis			
Other Similar Prevention Activities			
Appraisal Costs			
Sample/Prototype Preparation			
All Inspection Activities			
Setup for Testing			
Product Simulation and Development			
Vendor Audits and Sample Testing			
Maintenance of Test Equipment			
Quality Audits			
Maintenance of equipment used for quality enhancement			
Incoming and source inspection/test of purchased material			
In-process and final inspection/test			
Product, process or service audits			
Calibration of measuring and test equipment			
Code Inspections			
White Box (low level) Testing			
Black Box (high level) Testing			
Beta Testing			
Test Automation			
Out of Box Testing (prior to release)			
Other Similar Appraisal Activities			

Cost of Nonconformance	Man-Hours (avg burdened rate X total hrs)	Material (cost of parts/replacements)	Other Expenses (equip/depreciation, shipping, handling, not services)
Internal Failure Costs			
Scrap and rework handling			
Reinspection of rework			
Quality-related downtime (e.g. product holds, stop ships)			
Losses caused by vendor issues			
Failure analysis			
Inventory control and scheduling costs			
Downgrading because of defects			
Wasted Worker Time (e.g. waiting for parts, code, rework, doing work over)			
Re-inspection			
Re-testing			
Material Review			
Refurbish Activities			
Fixing Bugs			
Retesting Bugs			
Regression Testing			
Direct cost of late shipments			
Other Similar Internal Failure Activities			
External Failure Costs			
Loss of goodwill and future orders			
Warranty claims and adjustments			
Customer complaint processing			
Time & travel spent on customer escalations (including Executive time)			
Returned Goods			
Time spent on investigation of defects			
Product recalls			
Product liability suits			
Technical support calls			
Lost Opportunity costs (e.g. due to late ship, internal product issues, etc)			
Other Similar External Failure Activities			

Figure 3.9 Example data collection form for gathering quality costs

Cost Type	Q1	Q2	Q3	Q4
Prevention Costs				
Appraisal Costs				
Internal Failure Costs				
External Failure Costs				

Figure 3.10 Example summary spreadsheet to compile quarterly quality costs by cost category

Capturing the data is essential, but the real work becomes putting corrective action in place to drive down the failure costs, which should drive down the total cost of quality. You should hopefully start to see trends like the example in Figure 3.11 if your corrective actions are effective.

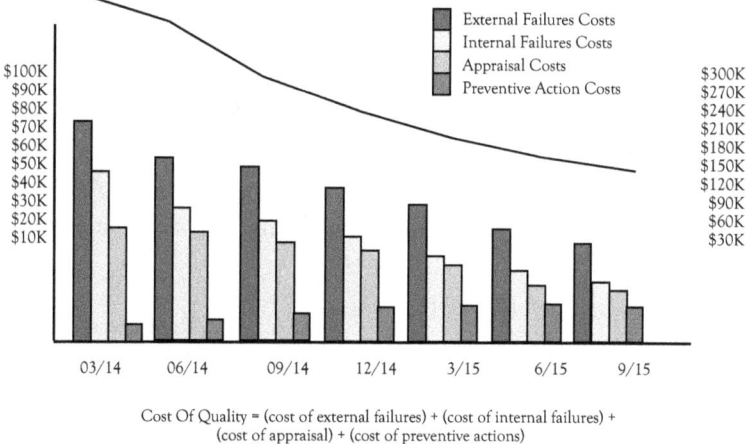

Cost Of Quality = (cost of external failures) + (cost of internal failures) + (cost of appraisal) + (cost of preventive actions)

Figure 3.11 COQ trends

You can eventually utilize this data to isolate and prioritize specific issues. In the example shown in Figure 3.12, we wanted to get a better understanding of the cost and trend of our product returns. But in doing so, we also found we needed to investigate why a growing percentage of the returns were determined to be No Problem Found (NPF) once they went through our failure analysis.

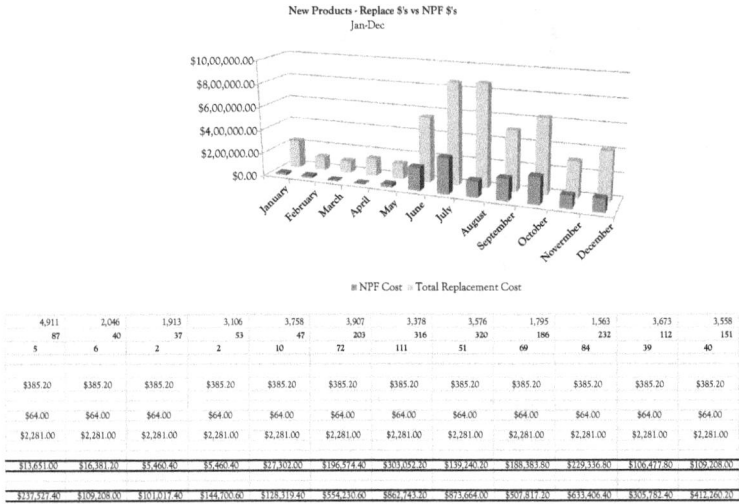

New Products - Replace $'s vs NPF $'s
Jan-Dec

■ NPF Cost □ Total Replacement Cost

4,911	2,046	1,913	3,106	3,758	3,907	3,378	3,576	1,795	1,563	3,673	3,558
87	40	37	53	47	203	316	320	186	232	112	151
5	6	2	2	10	72	111	51	69	84	39	40
$385.20	$385.20	$385.20	$385.20	$385.20	$385.20	$385.20	$385.20	$385.20	$385.20	$385.20	$385.20
$64.00	$64.00	$64.00	$64.00	$64.00	$64.00	$64.00	$64.00	$64.00	$64.00	$64.00	$64.00
$2,281.00	$2,281.00	$2,281.00	$2,281.00	$2,281.00	$2,281.00	$2,281.00	$2,281.00	$2,281.00	$2,281.00	$2,281.00	$2,281.00
$13,651.00	$16,381.20	$5,460.40	$5,460.40	$27,302.00	$196,574.40	$303,052.20	$139,240.20	$188,383.80	$229,336.80	$106,477.80	$109,208.00
$237,327.40	$109,208.00	$101,017.40	$144,700.60	$128,319.40	$554,230.00	$861,743.20	$873,664.00	$507,817.20	$633,406.40	$305,782.40	$412,260.20

Figure 3.12 Field returns

After digging a bit deeper, we found one of our larger customers to be the major contributor to our NPF issue, shown in Figure 3.13. This turned out to be a handling and training issue that we were able to address with them. Having this data available, made that improvement possible.

NPF Costs	79.14%
Fail Costs	20.86%

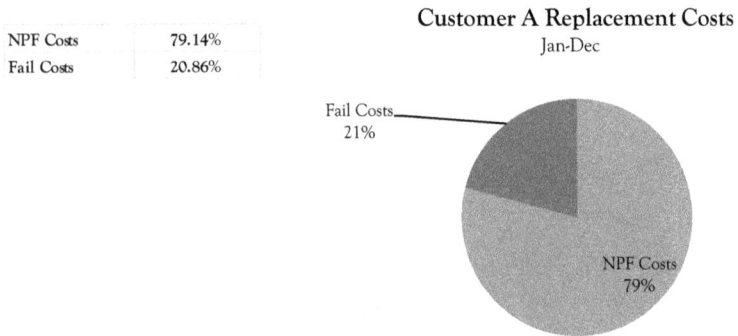

Customer A Replacement Costs
Jan-Dec

Fail Costs
21%

NPF Costs
79%

Figure 3.13 Customer breakout costs

The chart in Figure 3.14 shows the COQ from a program across its lifecycle. This was before we implemented a COQ program. The chart shows the costs by COQ categories. As you can see, not much time was spent on prevention.

COQ Category	Cost
Prevention	$3,173,243
Appraisal	$3,006,886
Internal	$6,013,771
External	$25,276,714

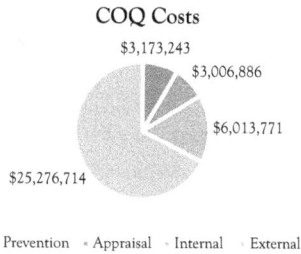

COQ Costs

$3,173,243

$3,006,886

$6,013,771

$25,276,714

• Prevention • Appraisal • Internal • External

Figure 3.14 Program breakout costs

For companies that do not have a strong metric system in place, COQ is a great place to start. It is an effective method for showing how the lack of quality is impacting your business. This approach provides a valuable structure for prioritizing improvement efforts. By monitoring the trends in this metric over time, you can better understand where to focus your efforts. Since COQ is using real dollars to measure quality issues and quality improvements, you can directly tie your results (both savings and costs) back to your bottom line.

Seven Basic Quality Tools

There is a standard set of tools associated with quality improvement, known as the 7 Quality Tools. These tools are intended to be a good starting point when first getting involved in quality improvement.

1. *Check Sheet.* A check sheet is a simple list of tasks to ensure no steps get missed. It can be used as reminder to complete each of the steps and the sequence they should be executed in. The check list can be used as a quality record, if there is no electronic record kept. An example shown in Table 3.6.

Table 3.6 Checklist for quality assurance

Number	Non-conformance	Corrective action	Responsible	Target Date	Status	Notes

2. *Histogram.* A histogram is a graphical display of data that visually helps you draw a conclusion. The data is typically based on a specific measurement or attribute and the frequency of occurrence for the different values. In Figure 3.15, the thickness of a printed circuit board was charted across several samples.

Row Labels	Count of Round Bare Boards
0	3
0.1	5
0.2	3
0.3	3
0.4	9
0.5	13
0.6	17
0.7	26
0.8	27
0.9	31
1	20
1.1	12
1.2	11
1.3	5
1.4	4
1.5	5
1.6	3
1.7	2
1.8	1
Grand Total	200

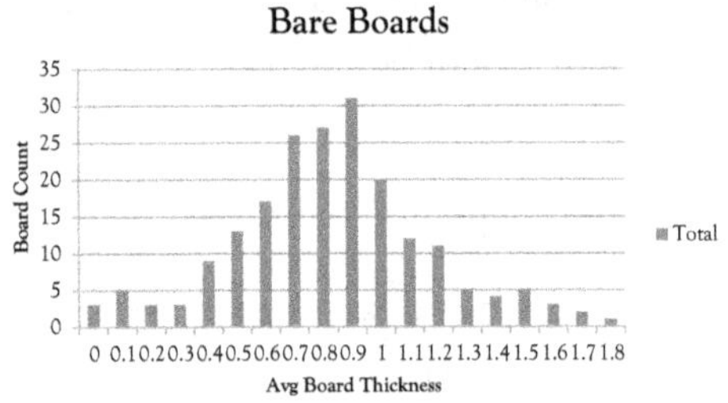

Figure 3.15 Histogram of bare boards

3. *Pareto Chart.* A pareto chart is another display of data that lines up the frequency bars in ascending or descending order based on frequency of occurrence. In Figure 3.16 the bars are showing the causes of test failures in descending order and the line shows the total accumulated failures.

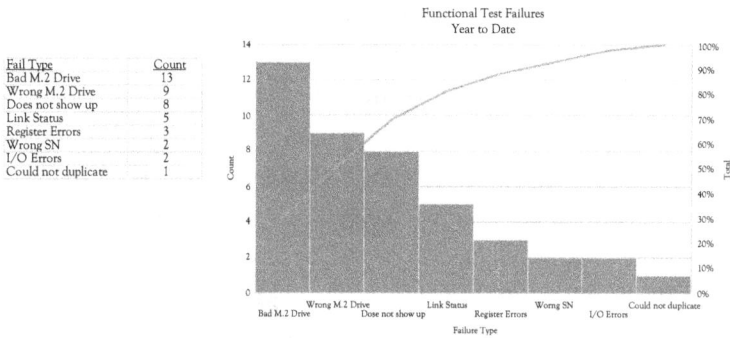

Figure 3.16 Pareto of test failures

4. *Cause and Effect Diagram.* A cause and effect diagram (also known as a fishbone diagram) is a team brainstorming tool to help identify possible causes of an issue or problem. You start by defining the problem you are trying to solve and place possible causes into likely groups. You continue to add detail by adding additional branches. In the Figure 3.17, the problem is High Product Returns. The failure groups identified are design maturity, vendor process, and internal process. Each of the failure groups get discussed. As more ideas are generated, more detail is added (shown as branches and sub-branches). For example, workmanship (under vendor process) has two sub-branches: poor documentation, poor training. You continue to add detail until the team runs out of ideas and suggestions. Then the diagram is used to develop improvements in the areas identified.

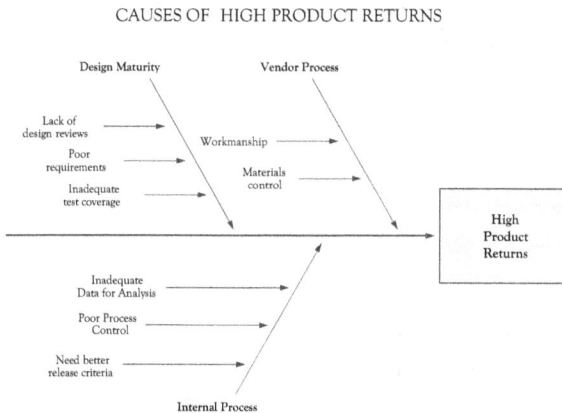

Figure 3.17 Fishbone diagram

5. *Control Chart.* The foundation for statistical process control was created by Dr. Walter Shewhart working in the Bell Telephone Laboratories in the 1920s conducting research on methods to improve quality and lower costs. He developed the concept of controlling variation and came up with statistical process control (SPC) charts, which provide a simple way to determine if the process is in control or not.

Dr. W. Edwards Deming built upon Shewhart's work and took the concepts to Japan following World War II. The Japanese industry adopted these concepts. The resulting high quality of Japanese products was directly attributed to the teachings from Dr. Deming.

Regarding SPC, there are generally two types of defects:

"Common Cause" defects. Common cause defects are those defects that occur naturally (i.e., "normal" variation) that is within established control limits. Common defects are what you might see from the day-to-day variation expected from a specific process. While you always want to work on reducing the variation, your process would still be considered "in control."

"Special Cause" defects. A special cause defect is an indicator that something has changed *with* your product or process. This would look like Lot #2 in the control chart in Figure 3.18, where you have a point outside the control limits. This is an early indicator that requires investigation. Examples include a supplier that made a process change, a supplier made a material substitution, a software engineer submitted new code without the proper checks, or a new assembly person was added to the line without proper training.

SPC is used to monitor processes and can be applied to both manufacturing and business processes. It uses statistical methods to ensure that the process is stable and monitors the processes for timely identification of special causes. All processes are subject to variation. SPC is used to help understand that variation and process capability. Control charts provide an analytical decision-making tool, which allows you to see when a process is working correctly and when it is not. Control charts also allow you to monitor trends. It is a good to see if your improvements are making a difference. While variation is present in any process, deciding when the variation is natural and when it needs correction is the key to quality control.

Figure 3.18 is an example of a control chart, plotting manufacturing yields.

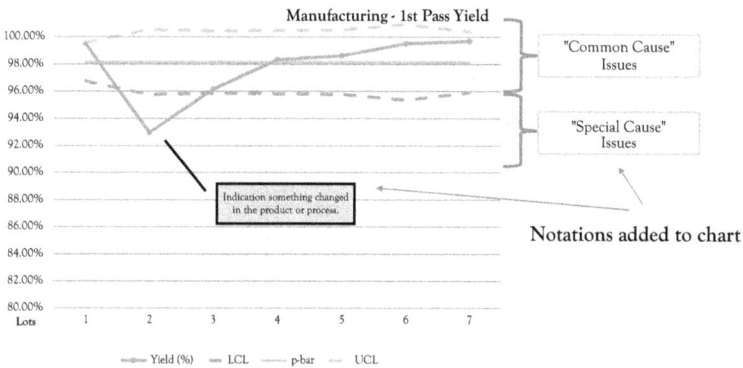

Figure 3.18 Control chart of manufacturing yields

The example chart is a p-chart that is used for monitoring yields and % defective. The p-chart uses variable control limits based on the sample size. This means as the sample size goes up, the limits (dotted lines) get tighter, which is why the dashes are not a straight line. Upper control limits (UCL) and lower control limits (LCL) are calculated from the data.

For the p-chart above, the data would look like Table 3.7. Notice the number tested (sample size) varies from lot to lot.

Control charts are an essential tool of continuous quality control. Control charts monitor processes to show how the process is performing and how the process and capabilities are affected by changes to the

Table 3.7 Data used for p-chart

Lot	Date	Tested	Passed	Failed	Yield (%)	p	LCL	p-bar	UCL	% Defective
1	15-Aug	816	812	4	99.51%	0.00490	0.967362954	0.98151	0.995658289	0.49%
2	15-Nov	285	265	10	92.98%	0.03509	0.95757154	0.98151	1.005449703	3.51%
3	15-Jan	312	300	12	96.15%	0.03846	0.958630801	0.98151	1.004390442	3.85%
4	15-Feb	300	295	5	98.33%	0.01667	0.958177691	0.98151	1.004843552	1.67%
5	28-Feb	290	286	4	98.62%	0.01379	0.957778809	0.98151	1.005242434	1.38%
6	30-Mar	211	210	1	99.53%	0.00474	0.9536886	0.98151	1.009332643	0.47%
7	7-May	328	327	1	99.70%	0.00305	0.959195822	0.98151	1.003825421	0.30%

process. This information is then used to make quality improvements. Control charts are also used to determine the capability of the process. They can help identify *special* or *assignable causes* for factors that indicate something has changed.

There are two types of control charts. Control charts for attributes and control charts for variables.

(a) *Variable Data*

Variable charts are based on variable data that can be measured on a continuous scale. For example, weight, volume, temperature, or length of stay. These can be measured to as many decimal places as necessary. Individual, average, and range charts are used for variable data.

(b) *Attribute Data*

Attribute charts are based on data that can be grouped and counted as present or not. Attribute charts are also called count charts and attribute data is also known as discrete data. Attribute data is measured only with whole numbers. Examples include: Acceptable vs. non-acceptable, passed vs. failed, forms completed with errors vs. without errors, or number of customer orders with errors vs. without errors.

Table 3.8 lists examples of several types of control charts and when to use them. This is not an exhaustive list, but with a little research you can determine how to set up the right control chart for your processes, what data is needed, and how to interpret the results.

Table 3.8

Chart	Type	Use
u-Chart	Attribute	Defects per unit
np-Chart	Attribute	Number of defectives in a sample
p-Chart	Attribute	Percent of defects in a subgroup
c-Chart	Attribute	Number of defectives in a subgroup
Xbar-R Chart	Variable	Mean and range of a group (small)
Xbar-s Chart	Variable	Mean and range of a group (large)
X-R Chart	Variable	Mean and range of individual measures

The decision tree in Figure 3.19 can help to identify which type of chart to use, based on your process, sample size, and data type.

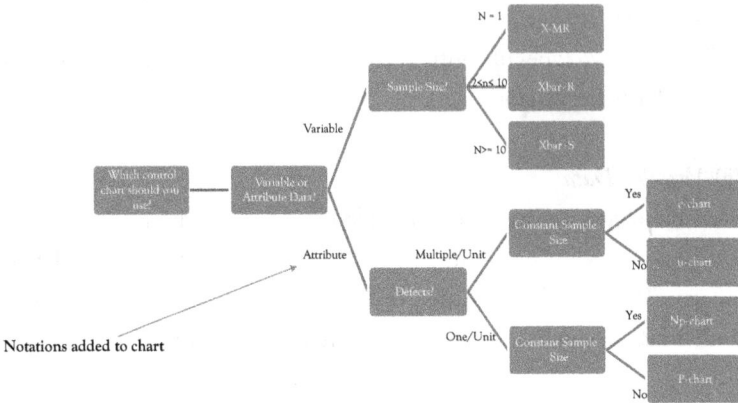

Figure 3.19 Control chart decision tree

6. *Scatter Diagram.* Another quality tool that can be useful is the scatter diagram. A scatter diagram is a graph, using pairs of numerical data with one variable on each axis. This plot of the points is used to determine if there is any correlation the two variables. The example in Figure 3.20 shows that more cold calls result in higher sales.

Cold Calls	Sales
42	$3,300
45	$4,000
49	$3,900
56	$4,400
63	$5,000
78	$6,100
86	$7,000

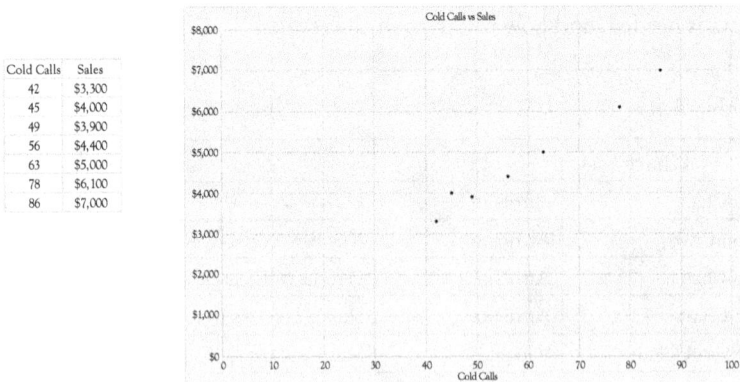

Figure 3.20 Scatter diagram for sales

7. *Flow Chart.* A process flow is a visual diagram that shows a series of steps to get a piece of work done. It typically includes a decision or multiple decisions, which can break the flow into different branches, based on the decision taken. We will discuss processes and flows more in Chapter 7. Figure 3.21 is an example of a high-level process for corrective action. In this example, issues can be identified from multiple sources: at the customer or in manufacturing. There is one decision point. If the cause of the failure is determined to be a bad component, then further failure analysis is required before determining the corrective action.

Corrective Action Process

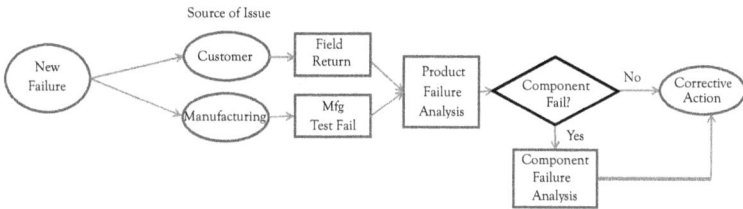

Figure 3.21 Flow chart for corrective action

Stratification
While I said there were seven basic quality tools, occasionally you will see a stratification chart as one of the seven tools. Just as a point of reference, it is worth mentioning here in case you see it listed as one of the seven tools.

Stratification is a method of dividing data into subcategories and classifying the data based on group, division, class, or levels that help in deriving meaningful information to understand an existing problem. When data from a variety of sources or categories are grouped together, it is difficult to visualize the meaning of that data. The stratification technique separates the data so that patterns of the data can be seen.

Other Tools

8. *Lean Tools.* The Lean principles are a comprehensive set of tools to drive improvement throughout a process or set of processes. Below are some of the key tools that help with Lean improvements.

5S. 5S comes out of the Lean principles and is a system for organizing spaces so work can be performed efficiently, effectively, and safely. Table 3.9 provides an overview.

Table 3.9

#	Japanese	English	Description
1	Seiri	Sort	Eliminate what is not needed
2	Seiton	Set in order	Organize by arranging and identifying for ease of use
3	Seiso	Shine	Clean the work area
4	Seiketsu	Standardize	Schedule regular cleaning and maintenance
5	Shitsuke	Sustain	Form a habit of following the first four S's

Kaizen. Kaizen is a Japanese term meaning "change for the better" or "continuous improvement." It is a Japanese business philosophy regarding the processes that continuously improves business operations and involves all employees. *Kaizen* views improvement in productivity as a gradual and methodical process. It refers to the practice of improving on a regular basis. The practice involves small, incremental changes rather than large changes. With Kaizen, all people within the organization look for possible improvement opportunities, not just managers or executives. The Kaizen philosophy is based off many Japanese management concepts, such as total quality control (TQM), quality control circles, and small group improvement activities with involvement from all employees. It requires a willingness to change and strong communication.

Muda (Waste). One of the best methods to increase productivity, save time, and reduce costs is to eliminate waste. The specific concept, within Lean, that addresses this is called *muda.* Muda translates roughly as waste and refers to the inefficiencies within processes which you can strive to reduce or eliminate entirely. Muda identifies eight key sources of waste (there were originally seven classic wastes, but an eighth one has emerged over recent years), shown below.

1. *Waste of transportation.* This is wasted movement of materials.
2. *Waste of inventory.* Costs associated with items not used in a just-in-time approach.
3. *Waste of motion.* This is the time and costs associated with the unnecessary travel around the factory or office.
4. *Waste of waiting.* This is when resources (people or equipment) are not being fully utilized because they are waiting on someone or a prior operation to complete.
5. *Waste of overproduction.* This is creating, building, and storing more than required for current customer demand.
6. *Waste of processing.* This is the unneeded steps in key process.
7. *Waste of defects.* This is the time and costs associated with any additional effort required when the work was not done right the first time.
8. *Waste of untapped or underutilized human potential.* This is the time and costs associated to an organization when it does not take advantage of the skills or talent available to them.

Poka-Yoke (Error Proofing). Poka-yoke is a Japanese term that means "mistake-proofing" or "inadvertent error prevention." A poka-yoke is a method or mechanism in any process that helps a worker avoid mistakes. An example would be to add a key and notch on two mating parts, so they can only be put together one way. Another example would be when using online forms, you are not able to hit submit until all required fields have been filled in. The purpose of poka-yoke is to eliminate product or process defects by preventing, correcting, or drawing attention to errors as they occur.

Value Stream Mapping. A value stream map helps to understand the customer's perspective of value. In this sense, value is any necessary step or action during a process of a product or service that the customer is willing to pay for. Refer back to our discussion of *muda* (the eight wastes), on where to look for non-value-added steps.

Value stream mapping is a Lean technique that helps companies visualize processes in an effort to define and optimize the steps involved in getting a product, service, or value-adding project from start to finish. When performed effectively, value stream mapping shines a light on ways to either reduce waste within processes or to increase items that directly add value to customers.

A value stream map can be divided into three sections.

1. Production or process flow. In this section, as in a traditional process flowchart, the flow of the process is drawn from left to right.
2. Information or communication flow. In this section all the communication that occurs within the value stream is shown. Note that communication can flow in any direction.
3. Timelines and travel distances. Timelines appear at the bottom of the value stream map. This conveys the time-related data measured in the process improvement.

9. *Failure Mode and Effects Analysis.*

Developed in the 1940s by the U.S. military, failure modes and effects analysis (FMEA) is a structured approach for identifying possible failures in a design, a manufacturing or assembly process, or in a product or service.

- **Failure modes.** The ways or modes, in which something might fail. Failures are any errors or defects, especially ones that affect the customer, and can be potential or actual.
- **Effects analysis.** Refers to studying the consequences of those failures.

Failures are prioritized according to how serious their consequences are, how frequently they occur, and how easily they can be detected. The purpose of the FMEA is to take action toward the elimination or reduction of failures, starting with the highest-priority ones. The information can be collected in a simple spreadsheet that might include:

- Product function
- Function owner

- Potential failure mode
- Potential effect of failure
- Likely severity
- Potential cause of failure
- Probability of occurrence
- Detection capability
- Recommended action

10. *Risk Prioritization Number.*
The risk prioritization number (RPN) is a structured method for assigning risk to issues. It is particularly useful, when you have a number of issues and need to prioritize which ones should be addressed first. It is based on a multiple of the three values outlined below. It is intended to be a formal mechanism / methodology for prioritizing issues and quantifying the associated risks to the customer, and ultimately the business.

The RPN Formula Is: RPN = "S" × "O" × "D"

As a general rule, the higher the RPN value, the higher the risk to the customer / business and the more critical it becomes to ensure the issue's resolution.

(i)   *Value "S": Issue Severity / Impact*
Severity 1 (Priority=Critical). Product, service, process, or function is non-operational or there is a direct safety threat to the personnel, product, or the environment. The system or product is not operational resulting in a critical impact to the customer's business, requiring immediate resolution. Weight = 5

Severity 2 (Priority=Major). Product, service, process, or function is severely degraded. The system or product is operational, but with severely restricted functionality or system degradation that impacts the customer's business (addresses degraded functionality of a product). Weight = 3

Severity 3 (Priority=Minor). Product, service, process, or function is operational with impaired capability. The system or product is operational

with functional limitations or restrictions to the overall customer operations (potential impact to customer with limitations to expected functionality). Weight = 1

(ii)   *Value "O": Predicted Likelihood of Occurrence*
High. High probability to occur during normal conditions (system is
being operated within published specifications / limits / configurations).
Weight = 5

Moderate. Moderate probability to occur during normal conditions (system is being operated within published specifications / limits / configurations). Weight = 3

Low. Low probability to occur during normal conditions (system is
being operated within published specifications / limits / configurations).
Weight = 1

(iii)   *Value "D": Ability to Detect and Mitigate Without Customer
Knowledge / Impact*

High. High probability that customer will be aware of the issue or they
will be required to take action to remediate it. Weight = 5

Moderate. Moderate probability that customer will be aware of the issue
or they will be required to take action to remediate it. Weight = 3

Low. Low probability that customer will be aware of the issue or they will
be required to take action to remediate it. Weight = 1

RPN is a good way to manage risks. At one of the startups I worked
at, we wanted to prioritize our backlog of issues in preparation for the
initial release of our new product. It helped us determine which issues
would be addressed in the planned builds leading up to the final release
build, based on impact of the issue, along with availability of engineering
and test resources. Figure 3.22 shows an example of tracking this in a
spreadsheet.

Ticket #	Issue	Priority	Likelihood	Impact	RPN	Status
629	Fatal error detected	major	low	high	15	fixed
823	Read data mismatch	critical	med	high	75	assigned

Figure 3.22 Spreadsheet for RPN

Training

Continuous improvement is very dependent on continuous learning. Improvement is based on what we are learning about our products, processes, and people. Within the context of this book, there is a wide range of learning needs, to include:

- Management and leadership training
- Change management training
- Program management training
- Educating teams on the quality strategy, vision, and goals
- Educating teams on the quality methods and tools
- Information and wisdom to come out of the data analysis efforts
- Lessons learned from the improvement efforts

Training is about making an investment in your team. The better the commitment, in terms of planning and resources, the better the return. Your training plan should take into consideration both general and individual training needs. For example, as you roll out the new quality strategy, it should be followed by training to help reinforce the key principles and train them on the methods and tools. This would be general training that everyone should attend (including management). There is also a need for individual training. This type of training is specific to an individual's role, responsibilities, career aspirations, and development needs. As a manager, it is your responsibility to ensure each employee, as well as the entire team, have the skills they need to be successful.

Determining Training Needs

Training needs can be built into the employee development plan. We will discuss development plans in a later chapter. But for now, here are some considerations:

- Know what skills you need to get the job done right (skills required).
- Know what skills you have on hand (current skill set).
- Develop plans to upgrade or recruit the skills needed to close the gap.

Delivering Training

Take advantage of the many ways that training can be delivered. Delivery methods can range from individual coaching to large classroom settings. Depending on the intended audience and material to be shared, methods could include:

- Classroom training
- Workshops
- Process or training guides
- Small booklets on a specific topic
- Computer-based training (CBT)
- Posting training materials on internal collaboration sites
- Mentoring program
- Individual coaching

CHAPTER 4

Functional Quality

Overview of Functions

Efforts toward quality improvement should be made throughout the company. There are quality practices and considerations that can be used in each business function to make quality better. Figure 4.1 shows a typical organizational chart. For each of the functional groups, we will explore areas where changes can be made to improve quality. Collectively, these types of changes improve the overall quality level of the company.

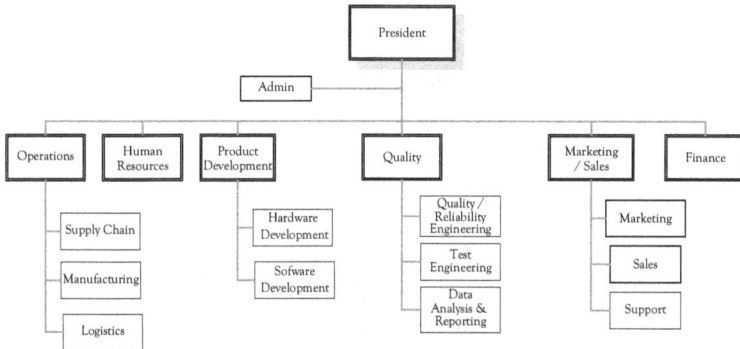

Figure 4.1 Organization chart

Quality in Hardware Design and Development

Designing new products is the lifeblood of most companies. Creating something new and innovative is what sets you apart from the competition. But what can the designers do to contribute to a higher level of quality? Start with the end in mind. Do not just simply develop an innovative product. Develop an innovative product that customers want and can be produced at a competitive price. Here are a few areas where the design team can contribute to a higher quality product:

- *Design reviews.* Design reviews are cost-effective way to avoid major issues later. But they must be done right. One or two people huddled around a white board is not a design review. Get the design out in front of a cross-section of people from different functions (with different perspectives). It's much easier and cheaper to fix something on paper than it is once the product is already developed.

- *Design documentation.* I am concerned that documentation has such a negative connotation. Too many development teams (in both large and small companies) avoid or even insist that design documents are not needed. I believe if you cannot (or won't) take the time to clearly document your design, how can you correctly develop it? How can you share it? There should be levels (or a hierarchy) of documents, from a high-level architecture down to the details of a subassembly or module. This doesn't need to be many, many pages. Just enough to effectively communicate with others. We will discuss this more when we get to testing.

- *Defect rates.* An early measure of product maturity (or immaturity) is tracking the defect rate during development. The key word being "rate," meaning it is measured over time. If defects are growing exponentially, the product is not showing signs of maturing yet. Not until the rate of discovery starts to level out can you say your product has started to mature. Of course, this also depends on the volume of defects you are finding and the levels of testing being used to find them. There is value in tracking the rate at which defects are discovered, as well as the rate that defects are closed. Understanding the gap between opened and closed helps you to understand when your product might be ready for the next phase of testing and eventually for release.

- *Design for X (DfX)—Design for Manufacturing, Design for Assembly, Design for Test.* Take the time to gather the appropriate input from other functions so that DfX is included into your design goals. Yes, it will take additional time to plan. But it doesn't do you much good to create an innovative product that is too error-prone for volume manufacturing. More on this under manufacturing.

Quality in Software Design and Development

In 2002, a study by the National Institute of Standards and Technology (NIST)[1] reported that software bugs are costing the U.S. economy an estimated $59.5 billion each year. Improvements in testing could reduce this by a third, or $22.5 billion, but won't eliminate all software errors. Jump ahead a few years. In a report on software failures, tricentis.com[2] found that in 2017, software failures cost the U.S. economy $1.7 trillion in financial losses (up from $1.1 trillion in 2016). In total, software failures at 314 companies affected 3.6 billion people and caused more than 268 years collectively in downtime.

To make significant improvements, we need to consider quality throughout the entire software lifecycle and not just the test phase.

The causes for poor quality software can originate from a variety of inadequate practices, including:

1. Poorly written (or nonexistent) requirements
2. Lack of acceptance criteria for all requirements
3. Poor coding methods (or poorly trained developers)
4. Lack of structured development methods
5. Lack of structured test methods
6. Poor integration methods
7. Individuals working on too many things (due to being understaffed or lack of planning)
8. Thrashing between teams as they try to integrate their work
9. Little coordination for how work is given to teams, expecting teams to self-coordinate

---

[1] Tassey (2002).
[2] Thorson and Wurst (2018).

10. Lack of alignment across the organization (i.e., across functional groups)

There is a definite impact from these issues. Typically, they result in some type of project delays, requiring additional time spent on:

- clarifying or rewriting requirements,
- finding bugs (fixing bugs does not take nearly as long as finding them),
- teams thrashing as they try to integrate various portions of code,
- working on the wrong things, due to poor communication or poorly developed specifications,
- fixing bugs,
- working on or removing features that are not useful (or would not have been selected had their true value been known), and
- working through complex code that is more complex than is needed.

The business benefits of including quality-oriented activities in all phases of the software development lifecycle are worth the additional effort. These activities will benefit the software effort by increasing predictability, reducing risk, and eliminating rework. They can also help to differentiate products from competitors. Most importantly, ensuring quality at all phases throughout the development cycle will always cost less than fixing issues after the fact.

In the article "The Software Quality Challenge,"[3] Watts Humphrey suggested that once you have tested software, you can only be sure that it works under the conditions you tested it. But as software becomes more and more complex, it becomes nearly impossible to test all possible conditions in advance.

In the book, *How Google Tests Software*,[4] the authors explain their approach toward quality. If a product breaks in the field, the first point of

---

[4] Whittaker, Arbon, and Carollo (2012).

escalation is the developer who created the problem, not the tester who didn't catch it. This means that quality is more an act of prevention than it is detection. Quality is a development issue, not a testing issue.

The key takeaway is that "find & fix," in and of itself, is not an effective quality strategy for software. Defect prevention should be the priority in any software project (remember from Chapter 3—"prevention, not correction"). In most software organizations, the project team focuses on defect detection (test) and rework (fix and retest). A major assumption in these types of efforts is that you will catch all or at least most of the defects. Elaborate testing frameworks are built and maintained based on this assumption. Except, what if your fundamental design is wrong or you are missing requirements? It is surprising how often defect prevention is either neglected or not the priority. It is more effective to take measures that prevent the defect from being introduced in the product right from the earliest stages of a project. While the cost of such improvements is minimal, the benefits derived are significantly higher compared to cost of fixing defects at later a stage. What if you eliminated the defects during the development phase? How much earlier could you release a product if you only had to run your test cases once?

Thus, analysis of the defects at early stages reduces the time, cost, and the resources required. The goal is to gather the knowledge of how defects get injected and then develop methods and processes that enable the prevention of those defects. Once this knowledge is put into practice, the quality is improved, and it also enhances the overall productivity.

Here are some practices that can significantly improve software quality during the development process.

Clear requirements. I cannot overstress the importance of good, clear requirements. The requirements need to be fully analyzed by the design and test teams, so that there is clear understanding and agreement on feasibility and testability. There is plenty of evidence that shows at least 20 percent defects built into a product are due to poor or missing requirements.

Design reviews. Just as with hardware design, software products need to go through formal design reviews with a cross-functional team.

Static Analysis. There are plenty of tools available to provide a static analysis of your software, such as code coverage and complexity analysis. Understanding and managing the complexity of your software can save time and money. Reasons for measuring complexity include:

- You can achieve *more predictability* in managing software projects if you know the level of complexity of the code being maintained.
- You can *lower the risk* of introducing defects into production if you plan for and manage software complexity.
- You can *lower software maintenance costs* if you proactively keep your software from becoming excessively or unnecessarily complex.
- You can *preserve the value* of your software asset and prolong its useful lifetime if you keep it from becoming excessively complex.
- You can estimate *when it is better to rewrite* code than to keep maintaining it.

Controlled Integration. Most software defects happen at the interface points, that is, where two software modules communicate or pass information. These interfaces are often more difficult to code and more difficult to test, especially when different engineers write the modules that need to communicate. Do they have the exact same understanding of the requirements? This communication is also more difficult when these interfaces interact with a user environment that is minimally understood or controlled. Extra care and time spent on these interfaces during design can reduce defects later. Development should be structured using a building blocks approach. Care should be taken to introduce unknown functions/modules systematically in a controlled approach.

ODC. Orthogonal defect classification (ODC) is a tool that characterizes defect data used in defect analysis. ODC was developed at IBM in the 1990s by Ram Chillarege.[5] It is a methodology that characterizes software defects and translates them into process defects. The intent with ODC

---

[5] Lyu (1996).

is to analyze defects to determine root cause of the problem. Defects are categorized by attributes such as defect trigger, defect activity, defect type, and defect cause. ODC is a great way of providing feedback into the development team, for learning and preventing the same types of defects in future releases.

In Figure 4.2, the chart shows the different defect categories that we identified at the top of the chart. Across the bottom are the different points in the development process. The bars indicate the count for each of the defect categories found at each point in the process. This is where those defects were discovered (i.e., defect trigger). The value of ODC is to look at what can be done in the previous step to identify the defect earlier. At SanDisk, we called this the "shift left" approach.

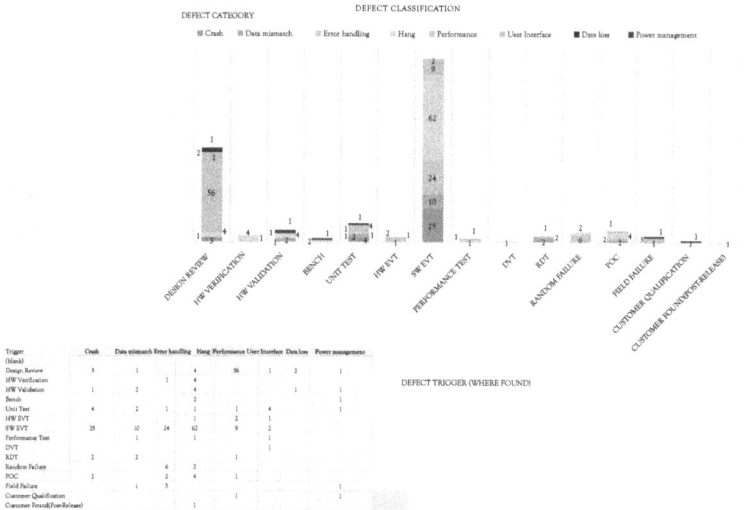

Figure 4.2 ODC chart

Quality in Sales and Marketing

Typically, most quality improvement efforts are internally focused, and the sales and marketing teams are not actively engaged. I think that is a mistake.

Sales and marketing are the primary interface to your customers. They should have the most knowledge about customer expectations and the relationships. That said, there are some very specific ways for sales and marketing to be involved in quality improvement. We will take a closer look at the focus on customers in Chapter 6. But here are some key activities that can help to engage sales and marketing in quality improvement.

1. *Voice of the Customer (VOC)*. VOC is a method for gathering information about your customers, in terms of their wants, needs, concerns, and business issues. The information can be gathered in a variety of ways, including but not limited to interviews, customer visits, surveys, focus groups, and feedback forms/e-mails.

2. *VOC to PRD*. The information captured in the VOC process then needs to be converted into clear product requirements. This usually takes the form of a Product Requirements Document (PRD).

3. *Response time*. Response time is always important to customers and it is measurable. Some customers require a service level agreement (SLA) to ensure specific response times are met for key items. Be clear on what is included and not included in your response time goals. It can include inquiries, request for quotes, sales order, fulfillment, follow-up, and response on issues/complaints. If whatever you decide to measure is inconsistent, take look at your process. Is there a process? Is it followed consistently? Is everyone involved trained on it?

4. *Forecast*. Forecasts are often difficult. This is especially true with small companies that do not have an established track record and new products that do not have historical data to work with. But forecasts impact many other areas of the company, such as the supply chain. How does procurement team negotiate the best pricing from suppliers if that cannot provide expected quantities? How can you perform capacity planning?

5. *Customer satisfaction*. Many companies do not formally measure and track their customer satisfaction. It is an important metric, but capturing the right data takes some thought. How do you determine the happy customers? Do you also follow up with unhappy customers? Lost customers? Make sure when you engage with customers for satisfaction feedback, the focus stays on quality and doesn't turn into a business development exercise. Keep these two efforts separate. Develop questions to see how they feel about your level of quality.

Quality questions around products, service, and the overall relationship are good areas to start.

6. *Monthly/Quarterly Quality Review.* A good way to build trust and confidence with your top customers is to plan regular quality reviews. These allow you to be more proactive, as opposed to urgent reactions to issues or problems. Partner with your lead quality person to show corrective action on previous issues, process improvement plans, data that shows trends that are hopefully going in the right direction. But if not, what you are doing to improve it? These types of reviews, if prepared for properly, can go a long way toward demonstrating to your customers that you really do take quality seriously.

Quality in Supply Chain and Operations

Supply Chain Quality

The supply chain has an important role in the outgoing quality of a product.

- *Supplier Relationships.* While it makes good business sense to have a backup supplier qualified for critical parts, there should be a primary supplier identified. The old style of managing suppliers was to squeeze them hard on price and delivery, then keep squeezing to drive down prices. That approach tends to build an adversarial relationship with your supplier. Is that really what you want? A better approach would be to develop a partnership, based on trust. Make sure they clearly understand your needs and you clearly understand their ability to meet those needs. Develop a relationship with them that benefits both of you. Treating them like a partner changes how you view them and also how they view you. Give them a chance to get to know your needs, your constraints, and your expectations. As you build these relationships, your suppliers are more likely to go that extra mile for you. What happens when you have issues? Or need something on short notice?

You are much more likely to get the extra effort from a "partner" than you would from someone you've been beating up on price. You should always be looking to reduce pricing and costs. Establish your goals and then work on them together.

- *Supplier Quality.* Even after building a partnership with your supplier, there still needs to be accountability. This can be done with a supplier quality agreement. This type of document gives the supplier clear criteria on what your quality expectations are. A supplier quality agreement should have metrics defined that the supplier agrees to meet. But it should also define what happens when there are issues, how they will be contained, and your expectations for corrective action.

- *Measure Everything.* Consistent with the theme throughout this book, measuring what you do is critical for improvement. Using the methods and tools we have discussed earlier, there are three categories of metrics that apply to the supply chain:

  o *Quality.* Determine what the critical quality requirements are, such as yields, defects per unit (dpu), defects per million operations (dpmo), mechanical tolerances, and set appropriate goals.

  o *Time.* Understand what time measurements will be important, such as cycle time, test time, lead times, on-time deliveries. Use the data collected to understand your constraints and drive improvements.

  o *Cost.* What are your high costs? Materials (pricing increases, scrap), process (rework, retest, reinspection, unnecessary operations), or people (overtime, training)?

- *Traceability.* Part of managing quality throughout the supply chain is having the controls in place for potential issues. It's not easy to predict what issues may pop up. But building traceability into your process is good mitigation to have in case something does happen. For hardware products, it might be tracking critical components to a subassembly and or final assembly serial number or date code. For example, what if you receive a bad batch of controller chips that get built into your final product? By having your traceability in place, you can "contain" the issue to a specific set of serial numbers or a range of serial numbers. Not having that traceability could be a nightmare. It could be the difference between recalling dozens of products versus hundreds or thousands of products. Traceability also applies to software, by controlling and tracking releases and revisions. This allows you to notify any customers that may have the release/revision in question and quickly send them an update.

Manufacturing Quality

DfX. As mentioned in the hardware engineering section above, DfX, or Design for X, is important for quality. The X can be for manufacturing, assembly, or test. Before you actually move your product into production, save your manufacturing group some significant time and headaches. Have them work closely with your development team to design the product with volume manufacturing in mind. It is great to have an innovative product that is technically unique, and a jump above the competition. But if it is a nightmare to build and test, you have severely impacted your ability to deliver your product. The more steps it takes to build your product, the more opportunities to make a mistake. Similarly, if you failed to design in the proper test points or test capabilities, you cannot design a comprehensive test, or at least one that can be completed in a reasonable time. These problems get incrementally worse as your volumes increase. Spending the extra time during the design phase, can significantly reduce your cycle time and the opportunities for mistakes.

Here are some considerations for design for manufacturing/assembly:

- Minimize parts: combine multiple into one if possible.
- Modularize multiple parts into a single subassembly. Make it easy to assemble/disassemble.
- Allow for assembly to be easily accessible for a hand or tool to reach/maneuver.
- Provide easy orientation for insertion of parts using self-locking or alignment tabs, or clear markings for easy orientation.
- Standardize parts to reduce variety (e.g., using same size screws throughout).

- Design parts so they do not tangle (e.g., cables) or stick to each other (e.g. washers).
- Distinguish different but similar parts from each other by color or some other means to easily tell them apart.
- Prevent nesting or stacking of parts.
- If parts do need to be stacked, design so largest/widest part is at bottom and smaller parts on top (e.g., like a pyramid).
- Design mating parts for easy insertion. Design in allowances to compensate for dimension variation.
- Design so assembly can be done from top-down. Never require a product to be turned over.
- Minimize the use of fasteners (e.g., screws), where possible use snap fit designs.
- If fasteners are used, keep them away from obstruction. Allow proper spacing for fastener tools.
- Identify critical components that need tight control and high quality. Consider vendor selection, process capabilities (internal manufacturing and suppliers), and traceability.
- For part selection, consider availability, lead time, planned end of life, vendor selection, and creating a manufacturing part number. Also consider temperature restrictions and board flex restrictions.
- For components, consider cost/quality trade-offs for pick and place versus manual insertion.
- Design for inspection: define specification limits, special tools/gauges.

The considerations in design for test depend greatly on the type of product, as well as the expected volumes. For high-volume products, you are more likely to invest in test development and tooling that will save you cycle time and improve test coverage. For custom one-off products, you may need a different approach. Whatever your approach, better to plan for the testing during the design phase. Finding out that your testing is inadequate or will require a design change during production will be significantly more expensive than designing the proper test capabilities into to the product.

Scale-Up Readiness

Looking to scale up a small business (or any business) can be both exciting and challenging. Often what worked for you in the early days or your initial release may not work as well at higher volumes. The stress of increasing volumes tends to break resources (people, processes, tools) if not carefully planned for. This can lead to missed commitments or defective products. Here are some suggestions, based on my experience working with multiple startups.

- *Developing scalable processes.* When you are starting out, a key person or two just know how to get things done. They work pretty independently and are able to make decisions on the fly. This is really helpful when you are starting out. But once you start growing and need more people to handle the volume, this approach becomes a problem. How do you know everyone is doing the work the same way? How do you know the decisions are being made consistently by different people? This leads to variation and a process that can quickly get out of control. Take the time to get your processes defined and understood by everyone. It makes it so much easier to scale.

- *Bigger customers demand more.* Starting out, just getting your product built and tested is enough for smaller customers that you hope to get feedback from. This works when you are dealing with proof of concept quantities. But once you start pitching to large customers and hoping to land some large orders, be prepared. Larger customers will want some assurances that you can be trusted to deliver—consistently. More importantly, they will want to see evidence. If you have put off documenting processes, collecting metrics, or putting a simple quality management system into place, be forewarned. This type of work doesn't just happen overnight—no matter how amazing you think your team is. Waiting until you land that big contract to begin this work will be too late. Do not blow a big opportunity because of a lack of planning and preparation.

- *Don't just think about development and sales.* Understandably, startups put plenty of focus on designing the product, marketing strategies, and proof of concepts. But even the most innovative products that fill a large need still need to be delivered. There needs to be a balance of resources between "product creation" and "product delivery." If you haven't prepared properly for product delivery, how do you expect to meet the demand? All too often I have seen so much attention (and resources) dedicated to development and sales. But when it comes to delivery on all those important orders, the operations team is set up for failure. If you have not staffed these functions properly, designed the product to be manufacturable, allowed them to fill the supply chain, provided them the tools and equipment needed to scale, how can you expect them to succeed? Once again, this is not something you can just "turn on" when you have that first big order. You should be building up your delivery capabilities at the same time you are developing your product and your sales pipeline. Make sure to allocate your resources equitably. Whenever there is an imbalance, it will cost you in quality, time, or both.
- *Don't forget about the support and administrative functions.* Scaling can break more than just engineering or manufacturing. Think about all your company functions and systems. Think about what happens when you ramp up customers, customer orders, and staffing. You need to make sure that hiring, onboarding, ordering, billing, payroll, and all the other supporting functions are ready for the ramp up as well. Do you have enough automation and resources to handle the expected growth?

Process Control

Measuring and controlling your processes is important in all areas of your business. But unexpected issues in your manufacturing process could have a significant impact on your business. So, putting the proper controls in place to prevent surprises is paramount. Putting controls in place goes back to our GQM methodology. What are your goals, what questions need to be answered, and what metrics will help answer those questions? For manufacturing, some basic metrics to consider:

Yields. Yields will tell you how your overall process is performing. After collecting some initial process data (such as during an initial pilot run through the process), you can calculate the control limits. Then plot your data daily, weekly, monthly, or by build cycles. Calculating yields for your manufacturing test, would look like this:

$$\text{Test Yield (\%)} = \frac{\text{Total Passed}}{\text{Total Tested}}$$

You can also look at the inverse of the metric, which would be the percent defective (% defective):

$$\text{\% Defective} = \frac{\text{Total Failed}}{\text{Total Tested}}$$

Rolled Throughput Yield (RTY). RTY is a valuable measurement, as it gives you a collective measure of all your manufacturing steps. Let's say your manufacturing process has these five critical steps, each with their own yield:

1. Post build inspection	95%
2. Bench test	93%
3. Postassembly inspection	97%
4. Functional test	92%
5. System test	98%

To calculate rolled throughput yield, you would multiple all these yields together:

$$\text{RTY} = 0.95 \times 0.93 \times 0.97 \times 0.92 \times 0.98 = 0.7726667 \text{ or } 77.27\%$$

This means your overall yield across the entire manufacturing process is 77 percent. This is important to know, because it tells you what your overall loss is for the entire process and how many extra pieces you need to build to achieve the final quantity needed. Here is an example:

Cost/ piece	Quantity Needed	Passed	Lost	Required Build	Added Cost
$100	100	77.27	22.73	123.00	$2,300.00
$100	1000	772.67	227.33	1228.00	$22,800.00

As you can see, this starts to add up quickly. If all you are looking at is your final system test yield, you may consider your yield to be acceptable. If this is the case, you are missing all the costs associated with the earlier steps.

Defects per Unit (DPU). DPU is useful a product can have more than one defect. An example would be at an inspection station, where a single product could have a scratch, a burr, and a wrong component.

$$\text{Defects per Unit} = \frac{\text{Total Defects}}{\text{Total Checked}}$$

So, if you inspected 70 products and found a total of 122 defects, your DPU would be:

$$122 / 70 = 1.74$$

Defects per Million Opportunities (DPMO). This is another common metric when a product or unit can contain more than one defect. For this calculation, you will need to know the total number of defect opportunities. A defect opportunity is the total number of possible defects. For example, if each unit can potentially have up to five defects and we produce 100 units, our total defect opportunities would be 500. To calculate DPMO:

$$\text{DPMO} = \left(\frac{\text{Total number of defects found in a sample}}{\text{Sample size} \times \text{number of defect opportunities per unit}}\right) \times 1{,}000{,}000$$

Manufacturing Readiness Review (MRR). Another method for managing and controlling your manufacturing process is to hold a manufacturing readiness review (MRR). This is similar to a release gate, to ensure all requirements needed for a successful production launch have been satisfied. This would include all dependencies or deliverables needed from both inside and outside the Operations team. A cross-functional team is used to review each deliverable and agree on the status. An example of a readiness checklist might include:

Requirements

- Design for Manufacturing (DfM) completed
- Design for Assembly (DfA) completed
- Design for Test (DfT) completed
- Mechanical engineering validation complete
- Electrical engineering validation complete
- Thermal analysis complete
- Assembly build time study
- New product design review with manufacturing/operations
- Manufacturing assembly instructions documented
- Manufacturing tools documented; samples provided
- Manufacturing test scripts updated for new product and verified
- Quality data plan complete
- Supplier quality plan in place
- Material review process defined to disposition defective/ obsolete material
- Packaging design plan in place
- Quality goals in place
- Agency/compliance testing is complete
- Environmental testing (shock/vibration) is complete
- Critical parts tolerance stack-up complete
- Supplier qualifications complete on new parts
- Capacity analysis for assembly is complete
- Capacity analysis for test is complete
- Manufacturing build pilot complete
- Manufacturing test pilot complete

As part of controlling the manufacturing process, you may periodically schedule a full or partial readiness review when there are changes made to the product or the manufacturing process. Examples of product and process changes could be:

- New or updated product software
- New supplier for a critical component or assembly
- Changes to the test process or tools

There are several different ways to trigger another MRR. Some examples would be:

- Design reviews
- Engineering changes to a product, software, assembly fixture, manufacturing process, packaging or the bill of materials (BOM)
- New testing software proposed for release
- New supplier to be added to approved vendor list (AVL)

Quality in Test Engineering

I stated previously in Chapter 1 that I believe it is incorrect to call a test function QA (short for quality assurance). It is very misleading in that it is such a narrow view of what the quality role should be inside of a company. But the term QA is so prevalent today, I do not expect that to change. Even though I feel QA as the only role for quality to be inadequate, that does not mean you can do away with testing. At least not until you have very mature development processes.

I have led many test groups throughout my career. But one particular development program stood out to me. This was at one of the larger companies I worked for, which happened to be very focused on total quality management (TQM) at the time. Early in the planning for this new product, I met with the head of the development team. I needed to put a test schedule together and was trying to estimate how many times we would need to go through our test suites before the product was ready to release. As we were meeting, we recalled that we found several issues in the previous generation product, as it moved from development to test (which was much improved from earlier generations where we found many issues after that transition). His response to me was, "Well, this time you won't find any issues. We will make sure it is rock solid when it comes to you." I'm glad I didn't make a bet with him, because I would have lost. We really tried to beat up the product during our testing and it was in fact solid. I think we may have found one or two very minor issues, but nothing that required changes to the product or reasons for us to rerun our tests. Just to set the context for this accomplishment, the product was far from simple. This was the third generation of a very complex product that included hardware, robotics, storage, firmware, and management software. It remains my standard for what can be done when you design quality in from the start. As you might imagine, the product released on time (zero schedule slips), because we never had to go through that vicious cycle of "find and fix."

I have always felt that testing needs to be tied to something. You need an anchor for your test development, so you don't end of up with a collection of ad hoc tests. How do you know if you are adding good tests or bad ones?

The structured approach to testing that I have been very successful with is called requirement-based testing (RBT). Through this approach, we can clearly identify the functions and features of the product and how to best test them. With RBT, we also want to fully represent the voice of customer (VOC), as best we can, by understanding the operating conditions and environments under which the product will operate.

The requirement process and its associated change control process are therefore absolutely essential to be successful with the development a product. This requires a very proactive participation of the marketing organization to make sure that the VOC, which represents the high-level requirements for the product, is expressed thoroughly.

In today's highly specialized world, it is very unlikely that an engineering organization is able to develop VOC requirements by itself, at least at the right level of detail. This is due to the fact that many products are integrated in very heterogeneous environments and have to cope with many different operational constraints. Therefore, the question of "what do we want to achieve with this product?" is more crucial than ever and requires a bullet proof process so that customer requirements can be successfully and efficiently implemented with feedback from multiple organizations. Without cross-functional feedback, the right questions may not get asked.

What Is a Requirement?

The first step toward understanding requirements management is to agree on a common vocabulary. Requirements in the context of product development are statements about the product (or service) you are developing. These statements should explain what the product is, what the product does, in what conditions or environments it should operate (or not operate). These statements should ultimately define what end user problem this product will solve or what condition(s) it will significantly improve. The success of the RBT methodology is directly proportional to the level of detail captured in the requirements. The requirements may start with the VOC, but should be thoroughly flushed out by sales, marketing, engineering, quality, and operations. Before development and test begin, you want to be convinced that the requirements clearly define the right product.

Benefits of Requirements-Based Testing

What makes RBT the right methodology for your business? If done early in a development program, you can expect the following benefits from RBT:

- Improved communication and increased accountability throughout the overall test effort
- An accurate scope of the test sizing through requirements analysis
- Requirement traceability through a documented requirements specification
- More accurate impact analysis for change management decisions with the requirements specification

- Efficient parallel testing, as a result of each group knowing their assigned requirements
- The assurance of test coverage and measurability of the requirements validation through the requirements scorecard

For RBT to work, a thorough analysis of the requirements is required. This involves breaking down each requirement into the lowest individual testable pieces and writing a test case for it. We called this "requirements leveling." This included both normal (expected) paths and exception (unexpected) paths.

A simple example is shown here in Figure 4.3.

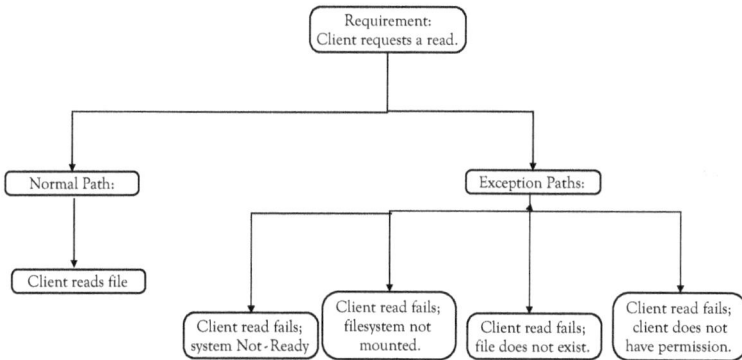

Figure 4.3 Requirements leveling

Another fundamental benefit of RBT is that it helps to answer the most common test question: "How do we know when we are done testing"? RBT allows you to answer this question by quantitatively measuring requirements coverage. Requirements coverage is accomplished by mapping test cases to requirements. This mapping provides traceability between requirements and the test cases needed to validate that requirement. So, when all the tests associated with a specific requirement have passed, that requirement can now be shown as complete. There is also the added benefit of using that traceability to manage control of your requirements and test cases.

If a requirement gets modified (as can often happen), you immediately know the test cases tied to that requirement need to be checked to make sure they still cover the modified requirement adequately. It can alert you that those test cases need to also be updated or additional test cases need to be added.

This method allows you track, in real time, how you are progressing with your testing activity. It makes charts like in Figure 4.4, easy to put together.

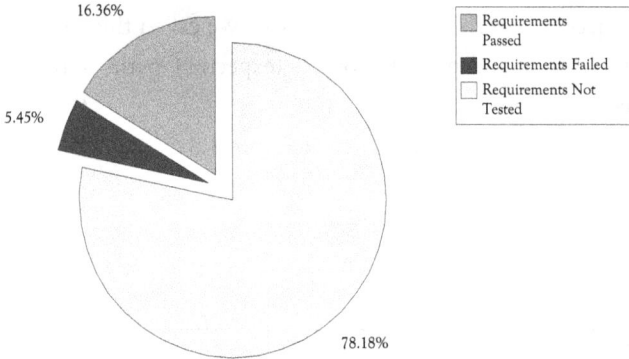

Figure 4.4 Requirements test status

We also built a scorecard that broke the requirements into the appropriate categories for better visibility. An example is shown below in Figure 4.5. The scorecard provides a method for assessing risk at any point in the process, by showing specifically the level of completion for each functional category. The scorecard can also be broken out by functional groups or individual testers, as well.

PROGRAM REVIEW PERIOD:							Risk Levels	
							High	0 - 49%
OVERALL TEST COVERAGE RISK:	27.47%						Medium	50 - 74%
OVERALL RISK LEVEL:	MEDIUM						Low	75 - 100%

	REQUIREMENT CATEGORIES							
Attribute	Reliability Req.	Performance Req.	System Req.	Usability Req.	Feature / Function	Support Req.	Customer Appn	Overall Totals
# of Requirements Originally Planned	10	25	15	21	44	12	22	149
# Changed, Added, or Dropped	5	3	1	3	12	2	7	33
# Final Approved Requirements	15	28	16	24	56	14	29	182
# of Requirements Passed	2	11	9	4	6	8	10	50
# of Requirements Failed	6	6	4	8	6	4	2	36
# of Requirements Not Tested	7	11	3	12	44	2	17	96
Coverage %	13.33%	39.29%	56.25%	16.67%	10.71%	57.14%	34.48%	27.47%
Risk Level	High	High	Medium	High	High	Medium	High	High
Requirements Churn								
Total Requirements Added	12	30	18	12	30	18	30	150
Total Requirements Changed	3	5	6	6	8	9	2	39
Total Requirements Dropped	12	4	10	12	4	10	4	56
# of Requirements Not Planned To Be Tested	3	10	5	3	10	5	10	46
# of Requirements Pushed Out to Next Release	3	5	6	6	8	9	2	39

Figure 4.5 Requirements scorecard

RBT drives more parallel testing, as a result of each group knowing their assigned requirements to be tested (as long as the entrance criteria for each test function is met). It is an efficient "divide and conquer" type of approach that makes the test coverage clear. This facilitates a very measurable test process.

Finally, this methodology enables communication between the groups involved in testing while keeping the required separation between those groups. This is one of the main goals of a key entity called the cross-functional test team within an end-to-end test strategy.

Key Point
Requirements coverage is not the same as *code coverage*. Code coverage is a measurement of which statements in a body of software (code) that have been executed through a test run, and which statements have not. Requirements coverage is a measure of which product requirements have been validated and which have not.

Testing Lifecycle

The testing lifecycle closely parallels the product development lifecycle. The testing lifecycle provides a functional view of the process that is followed for any test activity undertaken. This lifecycle is intended to be used by each of test group or functions involved in the test effort. The key process phases are identified along with the key activities and key deliverables for each phase. The duration of each phase varies depending on the scope of product(s) under test. So, this same approach could be used in agile or in waterfall approaches.

The objective of this methodology is to add a measure of discipline and consistency to the test services performed from test group to test group. There is one final point to make on using this testing lifecycle approach. The amount of time you spend in each phase is dependent on the size of your test effort and your specific needs. It is more important to go through the thought process for each phase than to spend days or weeks documenting it. Just make sure to build whatever time you decide is needed for each phase into your schedule.

Using this test cycle discipline enables a more predictable and repeatable testing effort and better management of available test resources. Other advantages of using a testing lifecycle approach include:

- To establish consistency in techniques, terminology, tools, improved communication, and strategy across the test groups.
- Investment in the upfront requirements and planning phases provides large dividends during the execution phase, in terms of efficiency and effectiveness.
- By utilizing the same methodology, test groups are more likely to develop and maintain efficient and effective test processes.
- A well-defined model provides a means for training and developing new engineers, as well as when engineers move from one function to another.
- A common model provides management with a means for resource and product planning, scheduling, problem solving, and decision making.

Although execution is the most visible phase of testing, it is important to note that execution is only one step of the overall test process. Adequate time should be built into each program schedule to allow test groups appropriate time needed for requirements analysis, test planning, and test development (test tools/cases).

The following phase descriptions are intended as a guideline. The example shown below is for a hardware product but could be easily adapted for software testing. Utilizing these phases in this testing lifecycle will help with the planning and preparation needed for a productive and efficient test effort.

Test Phase 1: Requirements

During the requirements phase, the purpose of the test is defined. This is critical to the success of the overall test process as the tester cannot anticipate results nor satisfy the customer requirements without clearly understanding the purpose of the test. The requirement phase is when the tester gathers the necessary information to adequately plan the test.

Also determined during this phase is the scope of the test. The scope sets boundaries around the test and specifically states what will and will not be tested, based on each test group's role in the overall test process. Other factors considered during the requirements phase include specific test objectives, product contracts, functional specs, and time frames/ schedules.

Key Deliverables

A decision on the feasibility of performing the test, the test definition and scope are established. Dependencies and impacts/conflicts with other projects are identified.

Test Phase 2: Planning

During the planning phase, the test plan is developed. The focus is on determining what is required to perform the test (e.g., equipment, man- power, tools, facilities, and training), expected results, test schedules, writ- ing appropriation requests for new equipment and risk/contingencies. As part of the test planning phase, the key assumptions and factors used as a basis for the test are documented in the test plan. A key part of the test planning process is the development of specific test plan and entry/exit criteria. The test plan is your roadmap to meeting your testing objectives, which should include purpose, assumptions, requirements, test approach, entry/exit criteria, and reporting.

Key Deliverables

Cost estimates, time estimates (test duration), entry/exit criteria, and the test plan are delivered.

Test Phase 3: Design

Phase 3 of the test process focuses on the actual test design. Depend- ing upon the nature of the test, this may include designing, reviewing, and writing specific test cases; designing and building tools; beginning product and new technology training; defining test metrics, and developing procedures for test execution. Development should be involved in the review of the test designs and test cases.

Key Deliverables

Test tools, test designs, test cases, test procedures, and expected results are prepared.

Test Phase 4: Setup

The first part of this phase of the test process is the readiness assessment prior to starting the actual test. Are all the facilities and power in place? Are the test cases complete *and* debugged? Are the units to be tested available? Is all the required functionality available? Is product training complete? Is the required test equipment in place and functional? Are all the necessary support functions (i.e., problem tracking system) and procedures defined?

The second part of Phase 4 is the dry run or baseline test. This is the first time all the pieces are put together and tested out (e.g., test tools, units under test, procedures). It is the last chance to make changes before officially beginning the test.

Key Deliverables

Test personnel are trained, and engineering contacts and test environment are established.

Test Phase 5: Execution

The test execution phase is when product testing begins. During this phase the tester executes the tests, manages changes to the product, detects and reports problems, works with support groups to resolve problems, and provides test status. The execution phase may include multiple test cycles, based on the number of code deliveries from Development. Each additional code delivery (after the start of execution phase) may require some amount of regression testing to ensure previously run tests still pass.

Key Deliverables

Test execution (new testing and regression testing), test status, defect reporting, metrics, and risk assessments.

Test Phase 6: Closure

The test report is issued that includes test results, deviations from the test plan, conclusions, and recommendations for product improvement. Note: the test report should map to the test plan. It should confirm your approach and assumptions. If your results do not match would you expected, the report should explain why.

Key Deliverables

A final test report is delivered, and feedback is requested. A lesson learned review should be conducted to assess the benefits of the test and recommend improvements for future tests.

Test Phase 7: Sustain

The sustain phase of a product involves assembling a subset of tests that assure the integrity of all functions during the engineering change process. Sustaining testing occurs after the product's release. As changes occur in hardware, system-level software, and firmware, the product is validated to assure reliable operation before release to customers.

Key Deliverables

Sustaining report and incident report are delivered.

V-Model

The V-model is used to illustrate how validation efforts align with the different levels of requirements and product specifications. Along the left side of the V, the different levels of requirements are shown. These requirements start at the top as high-level customer requirements and

they get progressively more detailed as you move toward the bottom portion of the V where it is more likely to be low-level design specifications.
The right side of the V illustrates the different levels of validation. Starting
at the bottom of the V are low-level functional tests, which could be a
specific function or component. Then going up the right side of the V,
validation efforts become more complex—meaning more variables and
environments are incorporated. The intent of the V-model is to show
how different levels of requirements are related to different levels of testing. This can be shown visually by comparing a requirement level on the
left to the corresponding validation effort, by going straight across the
V from left to right. This can be seen below in Figure 4.6.[6] These levels
of tests provide different test perspectives, each tied to different levels
of requirements, which can be coordinated through RBT. This results
in a more comprehensive test effort. From a timeline perspective, each
level of test is designed to build on the maturity of the previous level.
While some planned overlap between levels is expected, running these
phases in parallel can result in "thrashing" because the product may not
be mature enough for that next level of testing. Jumping ahead can waste
time and resources and usually causes a much longer overall test process.

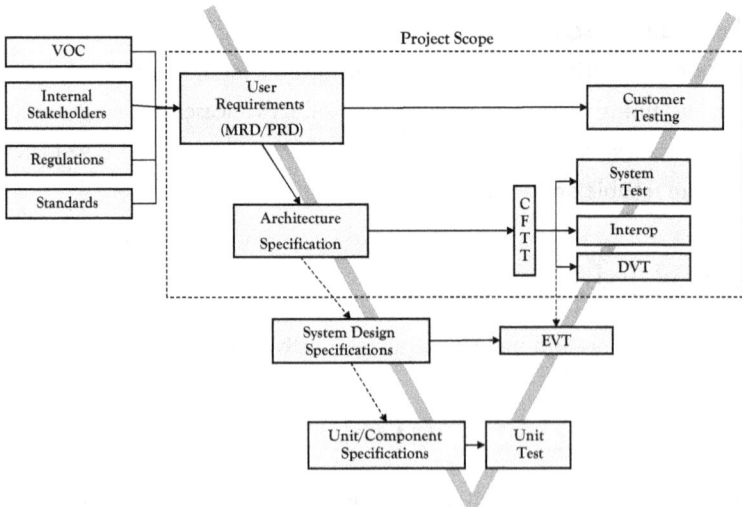

Figure 4.6 V-model

---

[6] INCOSE (2007).

Customers

Program Management

Analytics Team

Provides Data and Data Access

Customer Support

Quality and Reliability Needs

Defines Data Needs

Quality and Reliability Reporting

Quality and Reliability Reporting, Corrective Action

Customer and Field Issues

Product/People Cost Info

Quality and Reliability

Pre-Sales Data Support

Finance

Customer Sat Info

Sales / Marketing

Improvement ROI and COQ Info

Q and R Improvement Requirements Design Support

Quality Requirements

QA and Data Support

Engineering

Quality Metrics

Quality Support Needs

Mfg / Operations

CM's and Suppliers

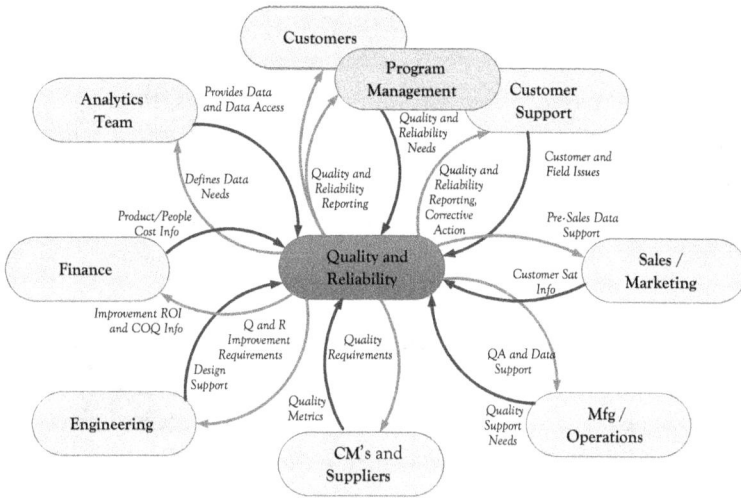

Figure 4.7 Quality and reliability engagement

Additionally, it is not helpful to the development team if multiple testers are reporting the same issues. This can be avoided by developing clear entrance criteria for each phase of testing and sticking to that criteria.

Quality and Reliability (As a Functional Group)

While I have mentioned throughout this book that quality should be everyone's job, there is still a need for a core group of expertise that helps develop, teach/coach, and lead the multiple efforts needed to developed and achieve that shared vision. The quality and reliability function should be highly visible and not buried deep under an engineering or operations function. In other words, they need to be seen and heard, as much (or more so) than the other key functions.

Ideally, a quality function becomes the hub that connects all the other functions together and leads everyone toward that shared vison of quality. This is illustrated in Figure 4.7.

Leading Quality

Leading quality today may be as challenging as it has ever been. As the workforce continues to turnover from generation to generation, much of the knowledge from the original quality gurus has been lost or forgotten. So have the lessons for developing a comprehensive view of quality that involves the entire company. In too many companies, the very aspect of using quality as a competitive advantage have been watered down to "testing quality into the product."

I think the biggest impact that someone responsible for quality can do today is to educate. How many companies know what their cost of nonconformance is? How many companies know how much time and money they could save if they really focused on the processes and training to do things right the first time.

Someone needs to have the knowledge and experience to differentiate between all the various acronyms that get tossed around whenever the idea of improvement comes up (e.g., TQM, LSS, CMMI, PDCA, TPS, COQ). There are so many ideas and methodologies to sort through. One size does not fit all. *Unfortunately, the decision on which method should be used for improvement is often decided by someone that has little or no quality experience.* The best approach would be to hire or bring in someone that has experience in all, or at least most, of these methodologies. Let them work through the type of process we have been discussing throughout this book and develop an understanding for the needs and issues. Then let them use their experience to develop a plan for improvement. What if TQM would be a much better fit for your specific needs than Six Sigma? What if a combination of methods would be best? Jumping into the *only* method you know of is like the old saying, "If all you have is a hammer, then everything looks like a nail."

There is an enlightenment that needs to take place before real improvement can start. The quality leader needs to create that sense of urgency. Until you have earned the legitimate interest of the executives, the models and methodologies do not matter. Crosby called this the "awakening" stage.

In his 1979 book, *Quality Is Free,*[7] Crosby introduced his quality management maturity grid. While many of his concepts are just as true today as they were back then, I have modified the grid shown in Figure

---

[7] Crosby (1979).

Measurement Categories	Stage 1 Uncertainty	Stage 2 Awakening	Stage 3 Enlightenment	Stage 4 Wisdom	Stage 5 Certainty
Management understanding and attitude	No real understanding of Quality management and what it could do for the business. If there is a Quality person, they tend to get blamed for "Quality problems".	Recognizes that focus on Quality may be helpful, but not a high enough priority to devote resources to it.	Start to show some initial interest in Quality. Could be the result from internal improvement efforts and customer pressure.	Management starts to recognize how quality improvement can positively impact the business. They get firmly behind the effort.	Quality Management as an essential function within the company.
Quality organization status	Quality as a function may not exist. If it does, it may be "QA" performing a test function, probably under engineering.	Likely view the QA team as the stop gap before product gets to customers. But the main emphasis is still on appraisal and shipping the product. Still likely part of engineering.	Start to invest in Quality resources to go beyond the QA function. Quality role has visibility beyond Engineering and Operations.	Quality Manager is a visible role in the company; works across all functions, quality information is shared across the company and reviewed regularly with executives.	Quality Manager prepares/gives reports to Board of Directors. Prevention is the main focus. Quality becomes a strategic advantage.
Problem handling	Problems are fought as they occur, no root cause; purely firefighting mode; lots of finger-pointing.	Teams are focused on addressing "showstopper issues." No deeper analysis is done to see if problems are related or systemic.	Corrective Action has been formalized, using a structured approach and driving to root cause.	Focus on finding issues early in the process. All functions work together to keep improving.	Processes, tools, and training have been effective and focus is on prevention. Rarely see issues now.
Cost of Poor Quality as a % of sales	Percent: 20-40%. COPQ $: $9,000,000	Actual: 18-25% COPQ $: $6,900,000	Actual: 12-15% COPQ $: $4,000,000	Actual: 8-10% COPQ $: $2,700,000	Actual: Less than 3% COPQ $: $900,000
Quality improvement actions	No formal improvement efforts. No real awareness of quality or improvement.	Focus is clearly "short term," addressing immediate issues only.	Education and training on quality improvement is started across all functions.	All functions are involved with the improvement effort and have the tools and training needed for drive improvements in their areas.	Quality improvement is now part of the culture and everyone contributes.
Summary of company Quality posture	"We keep having issues and don't seem to understand why."	"Having problems with Quality is normal"	"We are actively working on Quality improvement, we are identifying and resolving our problems."	"Our focus is on defect prevention and driving down failure costs."	"We know why we do not have problems with Quality."
For the COPQ example: $30,000,000 is used for Annual Sales Revenue example					

Figure 4.8 Quality management maturity grid (modified)

4.8 to have the explanations and impacts be more in line with current organizational structures.

As part of the modification to this grid, I have added a cost of poor quality example for each of the phases, As you can see, the better control you have over quality costs, the less you spend on poor quality activities.

Quality Versus Reliability

Although they sometimes get used interchangeably, quality and reliability are different. While related, there is a time element that separates them. The quality of a product is measured prior to a customer's initial use (as received). However, product reliability is measured throughout the customer's use of the product. Here are some distinctions:

- Quality is based on the present (today) while reliability is based on the future.
- Quality can be controlled and measured with accuracy, while reliability is based on probability. We can ensure better reliability by controlling the quality.

- Quality is everything before it is put into operation time(t)=0 hours, while reliability is everything that happens after (t)=0 hours.
- Quality is a static measure of a product meeting its specification, whereas reliability is a dynamic measure of product performance over time.
- You buy based upon quality. You come back and buy again based upon reliability.
- From a reliability perspective, there are three distinct phases over the life of a hardware product, shown in Figure 4.9. These three phases are typically referred to as the bathtub curve.

Infant Mortality. This is when the product is new and there can be early failures (i.e., manufacturing issues, weak components) that should be removed through maturity of your product and processes, before sending to your customer. A typical method for removing weak components and improving maturity is called "burn-in," where the product is run under stress (e.g., mechanical or temperature) to identify issues and drive improvements before shipping to customers.

Useful Life. This is when product has become mature and over the useful life of the product should experience only random failures (i.e., no particular pattern or trend) that occur within the expected failure rate.

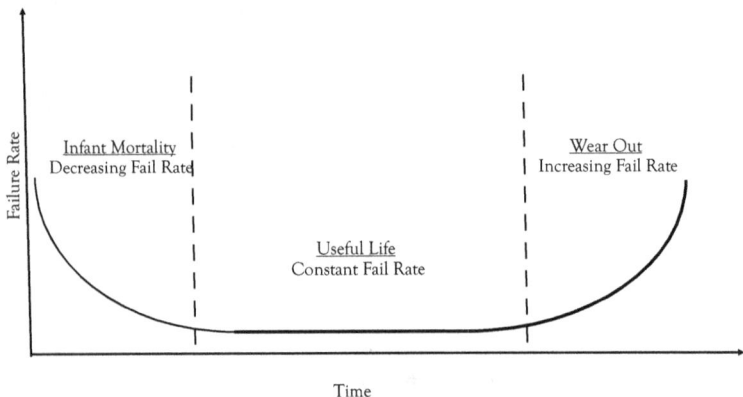

Figure 4.9 Reliability bathtub curve

This is often referred to as "constant" fail rate. The useful life failure rate should be significantly lower than the early failure rate and remain in that "constant" range, based on your design and processes. The exception would be "special cause" failures, that is usually due to a change in your design, supply chain, or processes.

Wear Out. Wear out, just as it implies, is when the product is reaching the end of life and parts begin to wear out. Understanding how your product follows this curve allows you to retire products before the failure rate significantly increases.

Hardware Versus Software Reliability

The primary drivers of hardware and software reliability differ in that hardware reliability, shown in Figure 4.10,[8] is driven by stress or wear applied to components that stimulate physics of failures; while software reliability, shown in Figure 4.11, is driven by changes to the product or process. This can include changes to procedures, requirements, coding, and test processes.

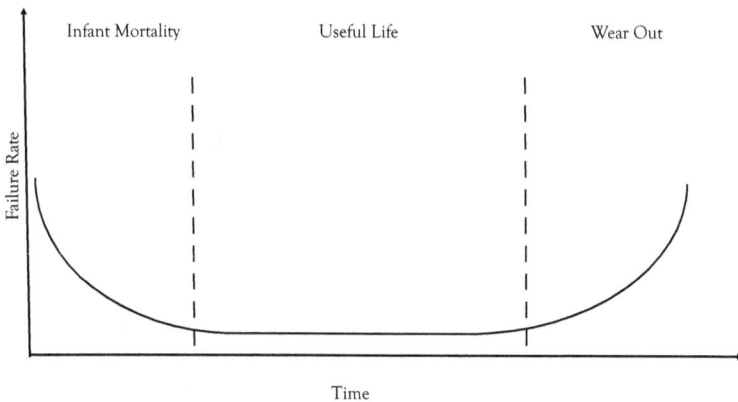

Figure 4.10 Hardware reliability

The spikes in the software reliability curve are typically tied to new releases or updates, as a result of the changes mentioned above. As these updates get exposed to the user base, there is often a small spike of issues

---

[8] Tobias and Trindade (1995).

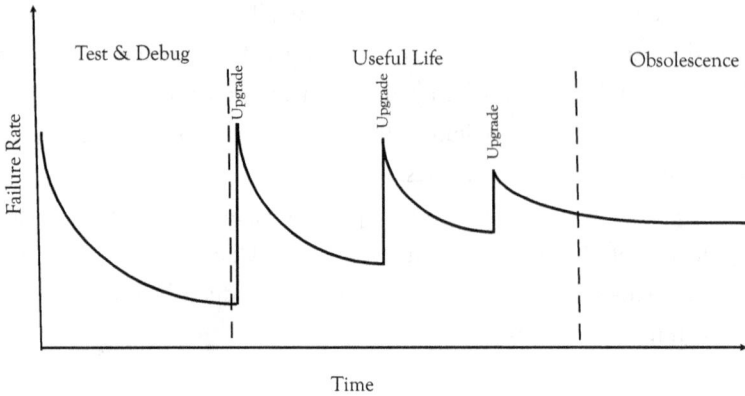

Figure 4.11 Software reliability

that eventually levels off until the next update. There is also the consideration that even when updates are available, it is up to the customer on when they will adopt them. While looking at updates is one view, it is also important to consider software reliability from a time to failure perspective. This looks at new bug discovery and the probability that a given product will fail over time.

Ultimately, the one common factor between hardware and software reliability is the dependency on good development disciplines.

Other Quality Roles

Quality Dashboards and Reporting. Once a quality vision and goals are established and measurements in place, sharing the information across the company is important. Using some type of online dashboard is an effective way to disseminate that information. More on this in Chapter 8.

Executive Quality Reviews. Having a standing meeting (weekly or monthly) with executives is important for the following reasons.

1. It provides an opportunity to share and ensure understanding of the dashboards and reports on a regular cadence.
2. Sharing progress on your quality vision and goals is essential to maintain executive commitment and engagement.
3. These reviews are an opportunity of to keep executives abreast of the top-quality issues (and the costs associated with them), as well as the

corrective actions needed, and any resources or assistance required to complete.

4. Any critical decisions or prioritizations that are needed to address corrective actions can be made immediately.

Corrective and Preventive Action (CAPA)

While all efforts should be taken to focus on prevention of issues, it is inevitable that some issues will still occur. This is especially true while you are early in your quality journey. Corrective and preventive action (CAPA) is a method for driving improvements into your processes. It is typically a component of your quality management system (QMS).

Corrective and preventive action aspects of CAPA have traditionally been connected, but there is a significant difference between the two:

Corrective action is the elimination of the cause or causes of an existing *non*conformity or undesirable situation in order to prevent recurrence.

Preventive action is the identification and elimination of the cause(s) of potential *non*conformities in order to prevent occurrence.

A CAPA process involves the identification, documentation, and elimination of the root cause of a nonconformity or problem to prevent the problem from recurring. A formal corrective action report is typically required under more intense conditions than a typical improvement. Some customers may require a formal corrective action report as a response to an issue they have experienced with your product or service. Most corrective action procedures use a variation of the 8D (eight disciplines) problem-solving approach. The following are the typical steps in a corrective or problem-solving process, such as eight disciplines (8D):

D1: Select a team—Select and establish a team of people with product/process knowledge.

D2: Define and describe the problem. Specify the problem by identifying in quantifiable terms the who, what, where, when, why, and how.

D3: Develop a containment plan; implement and verify interim actions. Define and implement containment actions to isolate the problem prevent it from reaching any customers.

D4: Determine, identify, and verify root causes and escape points. Identify all applicable causes that could explain why the problem occurred. Also identify why the problem was not noticed at the time it occurred.

D5: Choose and verify permanent corrections for the problem or nonconformity. Quantitatively confirm that the selected correction will resolve the problem for the customer.

D6: Implement and validate corrective actions. Define and implement the best corrective action(s). Provide evidence that the action(s) worked.

D7: Take preventive measures. Modify the management systems, operation systems, practices, and procedures to prevent recurrence of this and all similar problems.

D8: Congratulate your team. Recognize the collective efforts of the team. The team needs to be formally thanked by the organization.

Customer Quality Reviews. There are typically two reasons for holding reviews with customers. One is reactive and the other is proactive. Issues are going to happen. You may be requested by a customer or customers to explain why that issue occurred and what you are doing about it. That is the reactive approach—having a review when a customer requests it. Alternatively, you can establish a monthly or quarterly review with your top customers. These reviews take some time, but they are proactive in nature. You can use these reviews to show quality data on how your products/services are performing, including trends and improvements you have made or are making. This builds the relationship and builds trust. You can still address recent issues but doing so in a regular review cycle is less stressful on your relationship with those customers.

Quality in Customer Support

As a primary interface to the customer, Customer Support can play a key role in quality improvement and customer satisfaction.

Response Time

When you call a support line for any type of support for any product or service you purchased, you expect to get a quick response when you file a complaint on a product. Whether you talk to a real person or you fill out an online form, don't you want to get your question or issue addressed as quickly as possible? Poor response time is a big dissatisfier for customers. The only thing worse than having an issue with a new purchase you have made; it is going through multiple hoops to get the issue reported and resolved.

Decide what a responsible response time is for you and clearly communicate that commitment to your customers. Make sure that response time is achievable for your type of product and industry. Then establish a service level agreement (SLA) with your customers. Do not leave them guessing at when they should hear back from you. This is a key metric for customers. Be proactive and provide this information up front. Collect the data and strive to reduce your response times.

Root Cause Analysis

There is nothing more frustrating (or infuriating) than to have the same issue happen a second or third time. Root cause analysis (RCA) is critical for issues, especially those seen by customers. The only way to truly eliminate an issue is to determine the actual root cause of the problem and develop a fix or solution so that it never happens again. While the support team is likely not responsible for failure analysis, they can insist that the issue gets analyzed to root cause. They will likely have to explain it to the customer.

5 Whys. One simple approach to reaching root cause is the "5 Whys" method. By repeatedly asking the question "why" (five is a good rule of thumb), you can peel away the layers of symptoms, which can lead to the root cause of a problem. Very often the perceived reason for a problem will lead you to another question. Although this technique is called "5 Whys," you may find that you may need to ask the question more or less than five times before you find the root cause for your specific problem. The method is remarkably simple. Essentially, you keep asking why until you determine the absolute root cause. When you get to the point you cannot dig any deeper, you follow it through with a resolution that prevents the issue from recurring.

Quality in Program Management

A Program Manager's Role in Quality

A real-life example can help illustrate how a program manager (PM) can impact quality. Let's say we are developing a new product. The PM pulls together a cross-functional team to start the planning. The team consists of representatives from each of the functional areas. As the product requirements get rolled out, the team starts to create their plan. The PM works with each member to define their tasks and resource requirements and estimate a schedule for their portion of the program.

A rolled-up program budget and schedule are submitted to executives, based on time, cost, and resources needed from all the functional groups involved. The time, cost, and resources are based on a defined scope (i.e., product requirements) and hopefully an agreed-to standard for quality. Once the plan is approved, the program team moves forward with the development and release of the new product. The program now has an official start date and an official end date or release date.

But what if not everything goes as planned? What if the scope of the program begins to change, such as new requirements being added? What if the design was more complex than originally thought? So, now instead of taking 8 weeks for development, it may be closer to 12 weeks? What does the PM do? Were the risks previously identified with the proper contingencies built in? Do you push the out the release date? But what if you have already committed that date to a key customer? Or, multiple customers?

These types of situations happen all the time. It causes some ugly trade-offs. Do you cut back on testing to meet the committed date and compromise quality? Do you add additional test resources to compress the test time? Although this can also impact quality, by adding new resources that may not know the product and the test tools. Do you drop other features to add the new features and hope it does not create other problems? What if the product is complete, but the test team is completely overwhelmed with the high number of issues they are finding? Or, what if engineering cannot fix them fast enough to meet the schedule? There is no easy answer. The PM and quality lead need to quantify the risks (and the impact of those risks) and present a recommendation to management. At least one of these factors from the original plan will be impacted. Will it be:

- Quality?
- Scope?
- Time?
- Cost?
- Resources?
- Customer confidence?

These exact situations are where you really find out about your *commitment to quality*. Given these types of circumstances, the right thing to do is to give your team the needed time to do it right. If that means you have a tough conversation with your customers on previous commitments, then so be it. Be honest and tell them you ran into issues and the product is not quite ready. It is much better to be honest with them upfront and tell them product is not meeting your quality standard than it is to ship the product before it is ready. If you choose the latter and they find the issues, they will conclude that you have no quality standard. Or at the least, one that is inadequate.

Agile Versus Waterfall

There is an ongoing debate on two popular methodologies, agile and waterfall. Waterfall is the traditional approach that is based on program phases. However, more businesses are now moving to agile, which is intended to be more flexible and responsive.

A great comparison of agile versus waterfall was provided by Arnold Okkenburg.[9]

Agile Versus Waterfall Comparison

Table 4.1 summarizes some of the differences between agile and waterfall identified by Okkenburg.

Table 4.1

	Waterfall	Agile
Requirements Definition	Clearly defined requirements, reviewed before starting design.	Maintain a high-level product backlog and requirements defined as the design evolves.
Planning Approach	Emphasis on planning before starting design.	Plan progresses over sprints. Tend to defer planning decisions.
Scope Control	Scope is managed through control of requirements.	Change is expected as user needs change.

General Perceptions

Process. Waterfall requires too much paperwork and is a cumbersome process. The reality is that you can define a process that has the appropriate level of control desired and design a sufficient level of flexibility into the process.

People. Waterfall has no empowerment and agile has empowered and highly motivated teams. The reality is that you can create a level of empowerment that is consistent with the control and the capabilities of the team. You can use the appropriate management/leadership to maximize motivation in either model.

---

[9] Okkenburg (2012).

Customer. Waterfall emphasizes documentation over working software and agile emphasizes working software over documentation. The reality is you can develop a customer collaboration approach the balances customer engagement against control of requirements. Instead of creating documentation because that is what you have always done, use documentation to fulfill a real need.

Planning. Waterfall has heavy focus on following a plan and agile focuses on responding to change rather than following a plan. The reality is you can choose the level of planning for either to manage risks with an appropriate level of change control.

Some key recommendations from Okkenburg:

- Don't force-fit your business and projects to a methodology.
- Don't assume that you need to pick a single methodology.
- Don't destroy the methodology to fit a business culture that you know is dysfunctional.
- Do use agile as a catalyst for positive business change.
- Do tailor the appropriate mix of methodologies and practices to fit your business and products.

In my experience, I have seen both successful and unsuccessful use of waterfall and agile methods. As with anything, it depends the implementation and the people involved. For the sake of full disclosure, I admit that I have a bias toward waterfall. This is partly because I have more experience with it and many of the tools, I have recommended were designed for it. However, these tools can be easily adapted to work just fine with agile. I do have experience with agile development and I am completely confident that agile methods can work as well or better when the proper disciplines are adhered to.

Personal Observations

1. Agile works best when the development team is closely tied to the customer. When you have many customers and the development team has no direct connection or communication with them, agile has been less effective in my experience.

2. Even though agile is intended to be adaptable and quick to respond to changes, it is only as good as the discipline used by the development team. To this point, I have seen three major problems with an agile implementation and more importantly, I have seen this at multiple companies:

   (a) While agile is intended to be highly adaptive, collaborative, and have direct feedback with the customer, I just have not seen this in product-based companies. Maybe this works well when developing a website or custom software. But when you have a large or hope to be large customer base, it will be difficult for the development team to get direct feedback on portions of functioning code.

   (b) There is a disconnect when the development team is developing using an agile development process, but the rest of the company is working to a typical waterfall-like product development process (see Figure 4.13). So, all the program schedule deliverables are based on program phases, but the development team is working in a vacuum using their agile sprints. Nothing lines up exactly and deliverables get out of sync. This most often happens when there is a hardware component and a software component that makes up the final product. Most hardware efforts cannot adjust to changes as quickly as software can.

   (c) While agile is intended to be less about planning and more about responding to change, undisciplined development teams use agile as an excuse to not document anything. They *want* to work in a vacuum and be "left alone" to do their creative work. Look back to an earlier chapter that showed a real-life example of a product defect that cost the company $11 million. That issue came out of an undisciplined agile development process that was disconnected from other functional areas.

A pure waterfall approach is not without its own issues. As Okkenburg clearly stated, it takes the right balance of discipline and agility. Issues with the waterfall phased approach:

1. Putting so much emphasis on documentation and document control, bogs down the entire product launch process, not to mention creativity. You need to stop and ask yourself—"what is needed" versus "what do we want—just in case." Or ask yourself "do we need this because that's what is needed or because that's what we've always done"? The need for documentation should be determined by a cross-functional team. While it may not be important to the developers, it may be particularly important to functions like test, support, and operations. Do what is right for the entire program.

2. If you do allow yourself to get so bound by (unneeded) documentation, introducing a change becomes a time-consuming and convoluted process. Typically, when there is extensive documentation, there is also the requirement for lots of signatures. This quickly becomes the direct opposite of agile. So be specific about what is needed and how it is handled and streamline the approval process as best you can.

Process Gates and Checks

In those companies that do use a waterfall approach, the program manager (PM) is responsible for the phases and can contribute to improving quality by holding the program team to meaningful gate criteria. Typically, there is a gate review between each of the phases as shown below. Depending on the size of the company and the size of the project, you may choose not to have a review at every phase. Where there are gates, the PM can help to make sure there is valid criteria for each gate and that it is verified before a program moves on to the next phase. Allowing a program to move into the next phase based on a date is detrimental to your program and usually costs you more time and money in the long run. An example of program phases and program gates shown in Figure 4.12.

Work Breakdown Structure (WBS)

The work breakdown structure (WBS) defines the scope of the project and breaks the work down into components that can be more easily

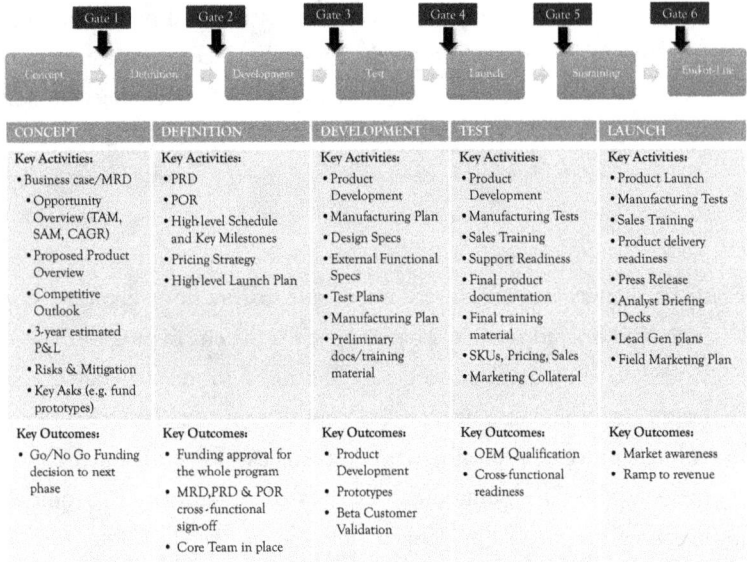

Figure 4.12 New product program phases

scheduled, estimated, monitored, and controlled. The idea behind the WBS is to subdivide a large complicated project into smaller tasks, until you reach a level that doesn't make sense to further subdivide.

From a quality perspective, a WBS can help to provide a more accurate and realistic estimate for getting work done. The PM can work with individual program members to create a WBS for their portion of the project. This helps the PM build a more accurate project level plan. An example WBS shown in Figure 4.13.

Resource Loading

Manage resources realistically. Don't load people up to 125 percent utilization and expect them to get their tasks done on time. If you want realistic schedules, be conservative when loading an employee's task time. Plan a resource to be loaded to no more than 80 percent to complete 32 hours of planned work each week (40 hours of capacity), or 6 hours a day. The other 8 hours that week would be spent doing other work that was not planned or isn't related to the assigned project (e.g., training, department meetings, administrative tasks, etc.). It all depends on your day to day work environment and how many things an employee must juggle.

Project Name:		Customer Satisfaction Reporting			Best Case	Most Likely	Worst Case
Task#	Major Task	Sub-Task	Responsible	Dependency	Estimated Man-hrs	Estimated Man-hrs	Estimated Man-hrs
1.0	Develop Survey Questions	Director Review			18	24	32
		Outside Consultant Review			1	2	3
		Executive Staff Review			2	4	6
2.0	Define Survey Mechanism in SFDC (Survey 1)	Group Questions			2	6	8
		Create Scripts for Delivery			0	0	0
		Schedule Survey 1			0	0	0
3.0	Identify Target Customer Lists & Schedule Survey	Create List			0	0	0
		Get List Approved			0	0	0
4.0	Marketing/Sales Review Board	Review Lists for Exclusions			0	0	0
	Execute Survey 1	Execute survey & collect data			0	0	0
		Data analysis			12	18	24
		Issue report			2	6	8
		Develop Improvement/Action Plans			2	12	16
5.0	Post Mortem on Survey 1	Compile Lessons Learned			3	6	9
		Create & Distribute Report			1	2	4
		Implement Improvements			8	12	24
6.0	Determine Frequency & Automate Survey 1	Develop Report Conditions			2	6	8
		Develop Scripts			0	0	0
		Auto-Load to DB			0	0	0
		Automate / Publish Reports			0	0	0
7.0	Define Survey Mechanism in SFDC (Survey 2)	Group Questions			2	6	8
		Create Scripts for Delivery			0	0	0
		Schedule Survey 2			0	0	0
8.0	Identify Target Customer Lists & Schedule Survey 2	Create List			0	0	0
		Get List Approved			0	0	0
9.0	Execute Survey 2	Execute survey & collect data			0	0	0
		Data analysis			12	18	24
		Issue report			2	6	8
		Develop Improvement/Action Plans			2	12	16
10.0	Determine Frequency & Automate Survey 2	Develop Report Conditions			2	6	8
		Develop Scripts			0	0	0
		Auto-Load to DB			0	0	0
		Automate / Publish Reports					

Figure 4.13 Work breakdown structure

Quality in Finance

If you choose to make *cost of quality* (COQ) your primary metric, it is essential for the finance team to work closely with the quality team to gather the data and present the results of your improvement efforts.

Cost of Quality. To implement a meaningful COQ effort, the right data needs to be collected and organized into the right buckets. The quality and finance teams need to be in sync on this. The worst case would be to have quality present their COQ findings and have finance disagree with the results. Both teams need to work together on the approach, data capture, and reporting. At a high level, there should be four main buckets: prevention, appraisal, internal failures, and external failures.

If this is your first time looking at COQ, I can tell you from experience, you are almost certainly not collecting all the data you will need. You may be able to pull together some prevention costs (e.g., design review hours, training classes). You may also have *some* of the costs associated with external failures (e.g., replacement costs). But for many of the costs, you will need new mechanisms to be put in place. This would include costs such as the hidden costs shown previously in Figure 3.10.

ABC for COQ. Many of the costs associated with COQ are based on activities. This could include value-add activities (e.g., developing a requirements specification), as well as non-value-add activities (e.g., retesting a

Planning	COQ Category	Total Tme	Std Rate	Total Cost
requirements analysis - any work around reviewing & analyzing requirements/specs	Prevention			
test planning/re-planning - test planning, schedules, writing test plans	Prevention			
test design - test design work, deciding how to test requirements, test design spec	Prevention			
test design reviews - holding or participating in test design reviews	Prevention			
product training - training required to test a product	Prevention			
resource planning - sizing the headcount needed for a test effort	Prevention			
equipment procurement - selecting & ordering equipment need for a test effort	Prevention			

Development	COQ Category	Total Tme	Std Rate	Total Cost
testcase development - developing/writing testcases & suites	Appraisal			
testing testcases - verifying testcases work	Appraisal			
automation - any development/scripting to automate tests	Prevention			
configuration setup & prep - any preparation/setup required to run a test	Appraisal			
test procedure spec - documenting procedural steps for running test/suites	Prevention			
test case spec - documenting testcases	Prevention			

Execution	COQ Category	Total Tme	Std Rate	Total Cost
execution of tests (1st pass of tests) - running a test for the first time on a new product	Appraisal			
regression testing - repeating tests you have already run on a new product	Appraisal			
fix verification	Internal Failure			
review release notes / workarounds - additional analysis or work required to work around problems	Internal Failure			
re-configurations - tearing down and rebuilding configurations	Appraisal			
field support - any work associated with supporting field issues	External Failure			

Reporting	COQ Category	Total Tme	Std Rate	Total Cost
gathering test status - effort required to gather daily/weekly test status	Appraisal			
reporting test status - effort required to compile daily/weekly status reports	Appraisal			
meeting & gate review prep - effort required to prepare for upcoming gates	Appraisal			
test reports - writing final test reports	Appraisal			
technical papers - writing technical papers (white papers, best practices, etc.)	Prevention			

Bug Management	COQ Category	Total Tme	Std Rate	Total Cost
problem recreation - time spent recreating a previous bug	Internal Failure			
failure investigation - time spent trouble shooting an internal problem	Internal Failure			
failure investigation - time spent trouble shooting an external problem	External Failure			
entering bugs - entering bugs into bug system	Internal Failure			
updating bugs - updating bugs into bug system	Internal Failure			

CFTT Management	COQ Category	Total Tme	Std Rate	Total Cost
planning - time spent preparing for and writing master test plan	Prevention			
reporting - any time spent gathering data and reporting status	Appraisal			
meetings - product related meetings	Appraisal			
bug management - time spent on bug management - internal	Internal Failure			
bug management - time spent on bug management - external	External			
schedules - time spent on building/updating/coordinating schedules	Appraisal			

Figure 4.14 **COQ time tracking**

product that previously failed). A method that can be used to tie costs to activities is activity-based costing (ABC). It would be nontrivial to convert your accounting system over to ABC if you are currently using a traditional accounting system. But there are aspects of ABC that can be incorporated with some basic timekeeping. This can be done in a spreadsheet to start and later incorporated into a simple database or time tracking tool.

In Chapter 3, Figure 3.13 shows a spreadsheet that captures time for the different activities within the four COQ categories. Multiplying the total man-hours times a standard salary rate for that position gives you a cost for those activities.

We used an internally developed database to capture time on the different activities for a test organization. We had specific activities that we defined, so we better understood where we were spending our time, in terms of cost of quality. The goal was to start putting more effort toward prevention and reduce the time spent on failures. Having the data in a database made it easier to summarize by activity, COQ category, by position, or even by employee. We developed a simple interface that made this quick and easy for employees to enter their time at the end of the week. The specific activities we used for test are shown in Figure 4.14. I worked closely with our finance person to set this up. I used the data to drive improvements in our testing and she used the data for her finance reports.

Improving Finance Processes

The other way that finance can contribute to improving quality is to look at their own processes. Much like quality, finance touches every function across the company. So, both the efficiencies and inefficiencies are felt by everyone. Here are a few improvement opportunities for the finance group to consider.

1. *Review your processes.* There are many processes used by a finance group (e.g., purchase orders, payroll). Walk through those processes. Is everyone involved aligned on how the process currently operates? If you are consistently getting questions on the processes, there is either a training issue or the process it too complex.
2. *Challenge the way it has always been done.* Don't keep doing things the same way, just because that is how it has always been done. Are there new and better ways to get the work done that are more effective and efficient?
3. *Reduce complexity.* Complexity leads to errors and mistakes. Look for opportunities to simplify. This includes eliminating waste, such as repetitive or unneeded steps.
4. *Minimize manual data entry.* The more manual data entry, the more opportunity for mistakes. Where you can, try to automate. But be careful. Make sure the process is solid before you automate. Automating a bad process, just results in creating errors faster.
5. *Minimize approvals.* For both small and large companies, waiting on countless approvals adds delay to getting things done. Do what you can to streamline the approval process. Set a goal for turnaround time and then measure it.
6. *Minimize deadline emergencies.* Accounting deadlines impact other activities. Try to plan for critical deadlines ahead of time. Develop a schedule and communicate it, so everyone knows in advance with deliverables are due. This should minimize those last-minute fire drills.

Quality in Human Resources

Human resources (HR) can play a significant role in quality improvement. Using the sustainable quality model, the foundation needs to be built on a culture of quality that embraces change. HR should own the process control for how that culture is doing. By that I mean, continuously monitoring and reporting on how the culture is doing and feeding that back to the management team.

There are all the standard responsibilities that HR is responsible for: talent acquisition, compensation, benefits. Those are all critical functions that are needed. But in addition, I do believe there are ways that HR can directly contribute to the quality effort.

1. *Culture assessments.* One way that HR can monitor the culture is to periodically use some type of culture assessment tool. Collecting and analyzing the data from these assessments can help you identify areas that may be drifting away from your desired targets. There are many culture assessments tools out there, from simple to much more sophisticated. You can decide how in depth you want to get with these assessments. I have created a culture assessment tool that aligns closely with the sustainable quality model. Please feel free to reach out to me to discuss further if interested.

2. *Training plans.* HR can help to take a global look at the training needs and help set the guidelines for how that information is captured and summarized. If there are high demands for specific skills, HR may be able to help coordinate cost-effective training across the company. For companies that want to be ISO-compliant, training records are a required quality record.

3. *Overtime.* Another area that HR may want to monitor is the amount of overtime being worked. This may vary greatly by groups and even individuals. While some amount of overtime is expected or even required, this needs to be managed so not to burn people out. Set up some policies or rules, so that individuals working long hours get periodic reprieves to rest and reload. There will be less frustration and they will likely perform better.

4. *Structured interviews.* I am a big believer in using structured interviews. Having a structured approach for how interviews are conducted will make them more effective and provide quantifiable results. What you put into interviews is what you get out of them. Very often in the tech world, people are so busy with their day to day activities, that they may not have the time to think about their interview until they are walking over to meet the candidate. Similarly, gathering feedback from the interviews in a timely manner can also be challenging. With a little pre-planning, you can have a much more effective interview process. We will talk about structured interviews more in Chapter 9. But this is certainly an area where HR can take the lead in setting up a consistent and effective interview process.

5. *Onboarding.* Another area where HR can take the lead is to establish a process for onboarding new employees. Hold the hiring manager accountable to have a plan. Create a checklist and make sure the new employee has the equipment and access they need. Make sure the manager provides the proper work guidance on what is expected over the first couple weeks. HR can help make sure all these items are in place *before* the new employee arrives.

6. *Turnover.* Anytime you lose an employee there is a cost. In fact, the cost to replace an employee can be as high as 50–100 percent of their annual salary. HR should work with the manager to get to the root cause of why that employee left. It may require digging a bit deeper than what is discussed on the surface. But to improve your retention, getting to root cause is important. Is your compensation not competitive? Are there not enough growth opportunities? Are the hours too long? Do you have a manager that is causing employees to leave?

7. *Career Planning.* Career planning ties back to the development plan in some ways. But development plans should be specific. Sometimes employees, especially those that are new to the workforce, just need help with the big picture. What are the possible career paths? Assisting an employee with some career guidance and coaching can help provide them with a sense of direction. Because they are not locked into a departmental view, an HR person may have a broader view of the workforce than a first level manager.

8. *Independent Employee Advocate.* Sometimes an employee just needs a safe place to turn to. Certainly, there are policies and procedures that need to be adhered to. But if there is harassment or bullying going on, an employee needs to know there is someone that they can talk to without bias or repercussions. There must be an element of independence between the HR and management. HR will not be trusted if they constantly side with management.

CHAPTER 5

Leadership

Quality of Leadership

As a young engineer, I was working in the quality organization. My department was responsible for doing a functional audit of our products after they came out of manufacturing. After a few years, I grew to become the lead of the group. I knew the products, the tests, and the audit process. So, when the department manager moved on, I got promoted to manage the department. I felt I had grown into the role and thought things were going well. That was until the director I was reporting to left and they brought in a new director from one of the top companies in our industry. As he started getting more involved, we had a few discussions and he impressed me as someone that really understood people, I assumed from his many years of management experience. He recognized that I was new to management and offered to help anytime I had questions or needed anything. A couple months passed and one day he called me into his office. He told me he had been watching me and decided he was going to make a change. I thought I was doing a good job but had no idea why he was watching me or what he might be changing. He said, "I've decided I'm going to move you over to manage the Safety department." "Safety?" I said, "I know nothing about safety." "Exactly!" he said. He went on to say, "I noticed every decision that happens in your department goes through you. All your people feel they need to check with you before they do anything." "It's time you learn how to lead. The safety team is very experienced. They can manage themselves. All you need to do is lead them." After I got past the shock, I knew this was going to be a major change for me. At first, I had no idea how to be useful. After a stressful first week of trying to learn who did what, I decided to sit down with the team and just be honest. At the staff meeting, I explained that I had no experience in safety and looked to them to handle the day-to-day work. I asked them what their concerns and issues were. What could make things better or more efficient? My director was correct. They absolutely knew how to manage the safety work. I listened to their concerns and issues and what typically got in the way of them doing their jobs. Based on our discussion, I began to focus on knocking down the obstacles we discussed, getting them better visibility across the groups they were supporting, and simply helping them individually to be successful. This change was my first "wow" moment of awareness about the difference between managing and leading. As it turned out, change was good for all of us. I was able to get them more visibility and support. I also got to know each person and help them individually with their career aspirations. It was certainly a great lesson for me, and we became a close team.

As I continued down my path of management, I wanted to continue learning and become the best leader I could be. So, enrolled in graduate school. My graduate degree is in the science of management. The degree program was very progressive and unique at a time when everyone was going after MBAs. It had a heavy emphasis on leadership and transformational change.

One night in class, our professor handed out an 8-inch piece of string to everyone in the room. His first instruction was to straighten out the piece of string in front of you (perpendicular to you). He then instructed, "Now take the end of the string closest to you and push it across the table, with no help from your other hand." As you can imagine, everyone struggled to make any progress. The string went anywhere but forward, as the professor watched unsurprised. After a few minutes, he said "Stop!" "Now, straighten out the string in front of you again," he said. Then he instructed, "Now, grab the end of the string farthest away from you and pull the string to the end of the table." Of course, everyone accomplished this in seconds. He then went on to explain the point of the two exercises. The first exercise represented the old philosophy of management, where managers were told to push their employees to make sure their work got done. The point of second exercise was the contrast between management and leadership, where leading your employees is much more productive than pushing them.

These two simple exercises have stood with me throughout my years in management. As we went on to learn more about the differences between management and leadership, that exercise was my second "wow" moment of awareness. It inspired me to develop a better understanding of people and how to make them highly productive and successful. It has also created the desire to keep learning and stay current on leadership.

While these experiences certainly do not make me a leadership expert, they have no doubt made me into a better manager. If we circle back to how this ties into quality, I believe a "leadership" style of management fits exactly into the type of culture needed to build that quality foundation. Leading people, as opposed to pushing people, could make a significant difference in the type of culture you create.

Addressing Today's Management Problem

I believe there is a huge problem with how individual contributors get moved into management today. Since technical expertise has become the measure of success in most industries, promotion into management becomes a means for retaining top technical talent. Technical expertise is not limited to hardware or software. It can be financial expertise, sales expertise, nursing expertise, or operations expertise. I have spent most of my career in the technology industry, so I can say with confidence that this is the case at many tech companies.

Go back to my example of working in the quality department. When I got promoted to manage the group, I most certainly drove my team crazy. Since I knew (or, at least thought I knew) how everything should be done technically, I micromanaged them to do things the same way I would do them. I demanded more from them technically, than they were ready for. But the biggest issue was that nobody ever showed me how to be a manager. If you do not know any better, every problem becomes a technical problem—even when it is not. This happens every day in the tech world and not just at the first level of management. It happens all the way up the management chain. In fact, often the founders of the company were a few brilliant minds with an innovative idea.

I was truly fortunate that someone knew enough and cared enough to make me aware of this early in my management career. It made enough of an impression on me that I went on to get formal training in management.

I have since coached/mentored all the managers that have reported to me, so they do not make the same mistakes.

But who is helping all today's managers that get thrust into management because they were the most technical person in the room or in their organization? We are talking about some truly brilliant people (technically) that may not have a clue how to be a manager (or at least a good manager). And when the benchmark that everyone is measured against is technical expertise, why would anyone waste time learning about management? Just tell your people what to do and let them know when they did not do it to your expectations. Without some type of management training, most of them just do not know what they do not know.

Look back to an earlier chapter when we talked about software quality. Most companies today want to hire someone very technical to lead the software development and QA teams. I believe their selection criteria is upside down. Having a programming background certainly does not hurt. But what these teams really need is a good leader that understands the big picture and how to inspire people. A good leader can bring in the technical skills they may be lacking, to make sure coders are coding correctly. But if your software leader is down the weeds checking lines of code or creating testing frameworks, it is doubtful they are focusing on the things that contribute to that high cost of poor quality or building a culture that makes their team more productive.

One last distinction I would like to make, is the difference between an "untrained" manager and a "bad" manager. For the "untrained" manager, it is mostly a matter of getting them some formal management training, ideally before they are put into the position of managing people. For the "bad" managers that continue to use bully tactics of intimidation, you can expect that this approach will eventually catch up to them. It always does. Either they cross a line and have to be removed from management (or the company), or it greatly impacts productivity to the point where they are ineffective, and they cause people to leave. Any senior manager that allows or condones "bad" managers to operate this way are every bit as guilty.

Once again let's tie this back to quality. How would technical managers that are not trained in management impact quality? Think back to our list of demotivators that negatively influence your culture:

- Employees hating their boss
- Working in a toxic culture
- Overworking your people
- A lack of vision or how individual roles tie into a bigger picture
- Unclear expectations and poor communication
- Harassment or bullying
- Micromanaging
- Lack of or poor onboarding for new employees
- Lack of inclusion
- Treating everyone equally (when the performance is not equal)
- No consistency in how things get done or management continues to work around the agreed-to process
- Not addressing poor performance
- Management not following through on commitments.

How many of these do you think could be the result of an untrained manager that is completely focused on technical work, deadlines, and execution? How likely is it that these issues are contributing to a less than ideal culture, which in turn impacts your ability to have sustained quality improvement?

Leadership Versus Management

Leadership versus management? What is the difference? One of the main differences between leadership and management is that *leaders* have people that follow them, while *managers* have people who work for them. Another difference is that leaders tend to focus more on the future and

Table 5.1

Leader	Manager
Creates vision	Creates goals
Pulls team	Pushes team
Coach/mentor	Directs
Role model	Routine
Empowering	Controlling
Change agent	Status quo
Takes risks	Controls risks
Builds relationships	Builds systems

possibilities, while managers focus on what needs to get done today. The list in Table 5.1 shows the traits for a leader as compared to the traits for a manager.

Having a focus on leadership skills does not mean a complete disregard for management skills. The day-to-day work still needs to get done. That is part of being in a management role. The real difference between being a manager and being a leader is not so much about getting the work done, but how you approach getting it done. Rarely do I ever tell someone directly to do something. Unless it is an urgent situation, I always ask them. Or better yet, guide them toward what needs to be done with questions. Make it a dialogue not a monologue. I found that many times during these short discussions, the employee had a better idea or approach than I did, although they might not have got there without the discussion.

Clearly defining tasks, monitoring progress, helping the team with issues are all management responsibilities. The key is to view their success as your success. Do not let yourself get caught up in who gets the credit or the visibility. It should be about what the team accomplishes, and the manager is part of the team. Every person is motivated differently. Get to know them individually and what motivates each person. Try to rid your team of demotivators and find ways to make them excited about their role. Then help them when they need help, praise them when they go beyond your expectations, hold them accountable when they fall behind, and inspire them always.

I had the pleasure of talking to a former employee of mine recently. He was an incredibly talented and hardworking young engineer. We worked together in a very demanding and thankless environment. I could see the stress and demands were wearing on him. I came in each day, wondering if this would be the day that he resigned. So, while we were talking, I asked him why he lasted as long as he did. He told me, "It was because of you. I would have quit long before if it wasn't for you." I share this, not to pat myself on the back. I share this to show it is possible to create a bond with people, where they will fight through tough times with you, if they trust you.

Leading Change

The consistent theme throughout this book has been change. Whether you are considering a small change to one or two processes, or a companywide change, it can be overwhelming to know where and how to start.

Before change can take place, there needs to be a clear reason for the change. What is to be gained? Why is the status quo inadequate? What happens if we do not change? It takes buy-in for change to happen. If we look at this from within the context of the sustainable quality model, it is important to step through the phases in order.

1. *Quality culture.* You must prepare the culture for change. Remove the fear, doubt, and confusion. Create an environment where people are open to change.
2. *Quality strategy.* Create hope and inspiration. Help them to buy-in by giving them a vivid picture of what could be.
3. *Quality tools and training.* Provide them with the right resources to be successful.

Having led some large change efforts throughout my career, I can tell you that leading change is hard. No two change efforts are the same. So, there is no exact step-by-step process that works for every initiative. But the successes and failures of working through multiple change initiatives have definitely left me with some lessons learned. Keeping some of these lessons in mind, as you start your change journey, can help you to be more successful. Here is what I have learned.

Believe. If you are leading the change, it all starts with you. If you do not believe with all your heart, you will never convince anyone else to believe. Create a vision you fully believe in and then commit yourself to it 100 percent.

Support. If you are leading the change effort but you are not the one leading the company, then you will have to convince those at the top that the change is needed. Do your homework, make a compelling case that creates a sense of urgency, and sell your vision.

Landscape. Before kicking off a change initiative, you need to know the landscape of how this effort will be viewed. Who will be your supporters? Who will dig their heels in and resist? Who will be on the fence? Having some sense of the landscape before you start, will help you during your rollout and minimize the surprises. Have a plan for the fence-sitters and resisters.

Persuade. Understand the value your change will bring and be prepared to explain it. Most people will not have the passion that you do, so you will need to convince them. It is human nature to approach change with caution and apprehension. You will see this throughout the change effort. But do not confuse "persuade" with "force." As soon people feel pressured, you will have missed an opportunity gain their support.

Communicate. Throughout this change process, you must keep the communication flowing. The more people hear about it, the more they think about it, and the more it becomes less foreign to them. Be honest with your communications. Share the small and successes and the small setbacks. You will have both. If they see you are being open with your communication, you have a better chance of gaining their trust.

Teach. Do not pass up an opportunity to teach people about your vision. When you get asked questions or when you get challenged, treat those as teaching opportunities. The more they understand what you are trying to do and why, the better the chance they will support it.

Reinforce. When you do have those small successes, make a big deal about it in your communications. Keep reinforcing the value and impact of your vision. It is encouraging to those involved and may help convince those that are still on the fence.

Be Realistic. When you set your goals, make sure they are realistic. As soon as your effort starts getting some visibility and momentum, you will likely be pushed harder to do more sooner. You can be aggressive, but do not let that crossover into unrealistic. Push back when you have to and give your team a chance to be successful.

Accountability. When you do have setbacks or individuals that fall behind, make sure to deal with them promptly. Do not allow those situations to get worse. Understand what the real issues are. Are they juggling to many things? Is there confusion over priorities? Help them resolve the issues and help them back on track.

Dealing with Resistance

While change is inevitable, so is resistance to change. It is basic human nature for people to try to keep what they do and how they do it consistent. Sometimes those leading the change focus so intently on the expected benefits of the change that they fail to realize how the change will be perceived by potential resisters.

There are many different types of change. Organizations can change their business strategy, their use of technology, their organizational structure, their culture or any combination of these. Regarding sustainable quality, we are talking about changing to a new focus on quality. Understanding how to deal with resistance and barriers is the key to a successful change.

Expect that change will be met by some resistance in any organization. Continuous improvement means continuous change. As you lead the change toward sustainable quality, you should be prepared to deal with some level of resistance.

When I first arrived at Sun Microsystems, I joined a recently created division called Network Storage Division (NWD). At that time, NWD had multiple engineering organizations and a newly formed test organization. I was brought in to run one of the test teams. When I arrived, I found there to be very little formal test knowledge. The test organization was made up from various resources from other organizations across Sun. The group was technically talented and knew the products. However, most of them had never worked in a test role before. While they were still trying to figure out how to test, they were being either run over or ignored by the engineering groups. New products were going to customers with poor quality and the number of issues was becoming concerning.

Trying to get a feel for the scope of what needed to be done, I started meeting with each test group. I wanted a better understanding of what each team was responsible for and exactly what they were doing to meet those objectives. There were significant gaps, both in test skills and in test coverage. Although these groups were working hard and trying to do their best, the lack of test experience was holding them back. So, we started a training program on testing principles. I set up "whiteboard" sessions with each of the groups, with the intent of improving their test knowledge.

While going through these training sessions, I soon got assigned the task of putting together an end-to-end strategy for how to test and to ensure that we had complete coverage across a diverse set of products. I utilized my previous test experience, but also did extensive research on the latest testing best practices.

I personally managed a portion of the test efforts, with multiple test teams and an architect team reporting to me. I worked closely with my director and the other managers, so we all remained in sync on the vision and goals for the test organization.

In less than 12 months, the test organization had transformed from being ignored or run over to become a highly respected organization. We ultimately changed how products were developed (setting rules for how/when products could enter test), how we tested, and when we could release. The overall quality of our products significantly improved in this time. The improved quality increased customer acceptance and significantly reduced the number of issues.

Since Sun was a very large company at the time, both my manager and I started hearing complaints from other divisions about our new strategy. "That's not the Sun way" or "We don't do it that way" were common complaints. I remember being shocked at the time. How could something we had already proven was making a difference be met with so much resistance? The craziest part was that we were not forcing this on any other division. All we did was share what we were doing when other groups asked. Was it simply because our approach was different than the "Sun way"?

Because the attacks came from so many different directions and different levels, it took us some time to get our arms around it. But we eventually did and decided to lead with education. We believed in our approach and thought if we could show them the "how" and the "why" in what we were doing, maybe we could get some buy-in. And along the way, if we learned new methods from them, that would make us better too.

So, my boss and I got proactive and went on tour to start meeting with the different organizations. We tried to really focus on the "how," the "why," and the "results." We were careful not to imply this is how they should do it. Although were glad to spend more time with those that were interested. We never won everyone over. There were just some groups that insisted that the old methods were the right way. But we did get enough support from many of the groups, to the point where we created a test council to focus on sharing best practices.

There are several reasons why people resist change.

1. *Fear.* People are afraid that the change will affect the way they have always done things, or they just don't know what to expect.
2. *Trust.* There may be past resentments against management or the groups making the change.
3. *Uncertainty.* There is a personal uncertainty that they might not be able to live up to the expectations of the change.
4. *Loss of control.* People perceive that they will lose their control over things that previously they had some level of control over.

5. *More work.* The change may mean more work for them or they assume it will.

6. *Ego.* Some people in a position of authority may not want to admit they were wrong.

7. *Short-term thinking.* Some people may not see or understand the bigger picture or greater purpose.

To overcome resistance to change, leaders can apply the following strategies:

- Engage them. Involve the potential resisters in the change process, as best you can.
- Avoid surprises. Provide continuous communication about what's happened, what's happening now, and what's happening next.
- Move slowly at first. Allow people to ease into the change.
- Start small and be flexible. Bite off small pieces and be prepared for obstacles and detours.
- Create a positive environment. Be inclusive and understanding. Treat challenges as a teaching opportunity.
- Incorporate the change. Make sure small changes takes hold before moving on to the next one.
- Respond quickly and positively. Don't give issues a chance to worsen. Be supportive and confident in addressing them.
- Work with established leaders. Build credibility by engaging and aligning with key players.
- Treat people with dignity and respect. Whether people agree with you or not, always do the right thing.
- Be constructive. It is okay to challenge the status quo, but always focus on the issue and not the person.

CHAPTER 6

Customer Focus

Voice of the Customer

Voice of the Customer (VoC) is a process for gathering information about your customers' expectations, preferences, dislikes, and overall experience. There are several ways to gather this information, including directly through the sales team, focus groups, surveys, or shows and exhibits. This process captures feedback from your customers and potential customers. Some of it can be positive feedback and some could be in the form of complaints. But when it comes to their thoughts and opinions on new or future products, you will want to formalize that information into a set of requirements. Depending on the scope of your new product, requirements can be recorded into a formal document, such as a Product Requirements Document (PRD) and put into a requirements database.

Determining Customer Requirements

As you gather requirements, it is important to focus not only on the functional requirements, but also to include the nonfunctional requirements. Functional requirements are typically the features and functions of your product. These features and functions are what helps you *get* customers. But it is the nonfunctional requirements helps you *keep* them as a customer. Below is a brief explanation and example for each category. There may be additional categories for your product. Each category should be studied and defined as it applies to your product. These requirements may not explicitly come from the customer. They may need to be determined internally before designing your product.

Reliability. This defines how the product performs over its lifetime. This might include mean time between failures (MTBF) or annualized return rate (ARR).

Serviceability. Serviceability looks at the impact of repair or maintenance for your product. It is usually measured in downtime (how long it takes to fix and get running again).

Availability. For mission-critical products, availability is an important requirement. It is typically measured in "uptime." It is impacted by reliability (how often it fails) and serviceability (how long it is down when it does fail). It is usually measured in "nines." 99.99 percent (4 nines) equates to 52 minutes of downtime per year. 99.999 percent (5 nines) equates to 5 minutes of downtime per year.

Usability. Usability defines how user-friendly your product is to the customer. For example, it might include the maximum number of mouse clicks it takes to perform a particular action or function.

Performance. Performance is sometimes included in the functional requirements, especially if that is one of the key features of the product.

Interoperability. Interoperability is a measure of how well your products work with other products. This is usually defined in the form of a matrix, like a list of "what works with what." For example, you might see this with peripheral products that list which servers and operating systems they support. Interoperability is very time and resource intensive. The better you have this defined upfront, the better the chance to meet.

Knowing the nonfunctional requirements early and designing to them can save you major issues with your customer. At one of the companies I worked for, we developed a product that was intended to be high performance. When it released, it was in fact the fastest product in its class. However, we quickly found out that our customers hated how difficult it was to install. After many complaints, we had to make changes. We could have saved considerable time and customer goodwill, if we would have defined and validated requirements around the ease of installation.

Customer Satisfaction

Understanding where you stand with your customers is essential in building and maintaining a strong relationship. Ultimately you will have some feel for this based on new orders (happy customers) and complaints (unhappy customers). But as you look across your entire customer base, you want to have something that is more quantifiable. How much do they like you? Are there things the like and things they dislike? Are there areas that multiple customers like or dislike?

Capturing the data. There are multiple ways to gather the information from surveys, face-to-face, or social media. It's better if the survey or questions focus on quality, instead of tagging a few quality questions onto a sales questionnaire. Whichever method you use to get this information, it is important to collect it regularly, chart your progress, and use it to drive improvement. Put some thought into what you want to get out of this information. This is another opportunity to use a structured approach such as GQM (goals–questions–metrics).

Business/Quality Reviews. As mentioned earlier in the quality and reliability section, another approach that is more customer specific, would be to hold periodic reviews. This is more likely to be with key customers instead of your entire customer base, depending how big your base is. These reviews could be part of a larger business review, where you set aside time to cover quality topics. Or, you can hold a quality specific review. These reviews can be used to cover status on open issues, as well as provide an opportunity to talk about new improvements. These types of dialogues are a good way to gather the customer's thoughts and feedback, without the formality of filling out a survey.

Shows and Conferences. Many companies set up booths at shows or conferences to introduce their products. This is another great way to get some feedback in an informal setting. Maybe have a few questions on quality ready for customers or potential customers. Depending on how much time you can spend on these questions, you may want to have a quality team member present to show this is important to you.

Field Data. Tracking the performance of how your product does when it gets to your customer will critical information for you to know. If you receive a complaint from an angry customer, you should already know if that is a random, isolated case. Or, is this a trend you are seeing across multiple customers? If your return rate is getting worse, do you understand why?

CHAPTER 7

Process Focus

What Is a Process?

There is no product or service without a process. Whenever there is work that gets repeated to produce that product or service, you have a process. Whether you have it written down or not, there is a process. Processes do not apply only to manufacturing or production. They apply to all aspects of your business that have work activities (e.g., the order process, fulfillment, design / development, and support).

Before you can focus on process improvement, it is important to define what the process is. A process is the organization of people, equipment, procedures, and materials into the work activities needed to produce a specified output. A simple model shown in Figure 7.1 illustrates that a process starts with inputs provided by a supplier. Within that process, you take those inputs and change them into products or services. Those products or services become an output for your customer. The work activities that change your inputs into outputs are the steps in your process.

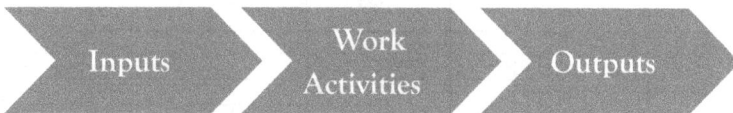

Inputs → Work Activities → Outputs

Figure 7.1 Basic process

Benefits of a Process Focus

- Documenting your process makes the activities repeatable.
- Repeatable activities become measurable.
- Measurable activities can be improved.

Defining a Process

Any process has five specific components to it. These components are:

- *Suppliers.* The supplier is function providing you what you need to start your process. It can be an external supplier, or it can be an internal supplier.
- *Inputs.* Inputs are the people or resources needed for your process, which come from your supplier(s).
- *Activities.* This is the work that gets done. It is a set of steps and decisions (i.e., a flow) that transform those inputs into an output.
- *Customers.* The customer(s) is who your output goes to once you have completed it. This can be an internal customer that continues to add value after you are done or it can be an external customer.
- *Outputs.* An output is your completed work once you have completed your required activities successfully.

A tool used to document this information for any give process, is called a SIPOC (Suppliers-Inputs-Process-Outputs-Customers), made popular with Six Sigma. Figure 7.2 shows an example of a SIPOC form, that can be created in a simple spreadsheet.

SIPOC					
Who are the	What do the suppliers provide to my process?	What are the activities/steps.	What product or service does the process		Who are the customers
Suppliers	Input	Process (High Level)	Output		Customers
1	1	Operation or Activity	1		1
	2	1			2
	3	2	2		1
2	1	3			2
	2	4	3		1
	3	5			2
3	1	6	4		1
	2	7			2
	3	8	5		1
4	1	9			2
	2	10	6		1
	3	11			2

Figure 7.2 SIPOC

As you start to define processes across the company, you may encounter some areas or groups that say, "We don't need to do a flowchart. The process is already in our heads."

There are three reasons why relying on the information "in our heads" is not recommended.

1. First, everyone involved in the process needs to have a common understanding of how the process works. If the process is kept "in our heads," it is entirely possible that each person has a slightly different view of how the work gets done. This is how you introduce variance into the process.
2. Second, to improve a process, you need to understand the exact flow of activities. It is highly unlikely that multiple people picture the exact same flow in their heads.
3. Third, as the business grows, new employees may be added to the process or responsibilities might change. Having the process documented, helps others get up to speed more effectively. It drives consistency and reduces variation.

Process Levels

To fully understand processes, it is necessary to know that they happen in levels. For example, let's say at the highest level we have two processes: product creation and product delivery. Let's call this process level 1. But these two processes can be broken down into sub-processes, such as in Figure 7.3.

Product Creation Process – Level 1	Product Delivery Process – Level 1
Level 2 Process	Level 2 Processes
✓New Concept Process	✓Production Readiness Process
✓New Product Planning Process	✓Production Ramp Process
✓Development and Test Process	✓Customer Support Process
✓Customer Acceptance Process	✓Product Retirement Process

Figure 7.3 Level 2 processes

Then each of the Level 2 processes can be broken down into level 3 processes. See the example in Figure 7.4.

Eventually, you will have a process hierarchy that shows how processes across the company align. Depending on the size of a company, defining levels 3 and 4 of a hierarchy is an appropriate start. This should provide a

Development and Test	Product Architecture
	Hardware Design
	Hardware Development
	Electrical Design
	Design For X
	Electrical Development
	Software Design
	Software Development
	System Integration
	Product Documentation
	System Test
	Engineering Change Management

Figure 7.4 Level 3 processes

clear indication of who are process owners, the customers, and the suppliers are for your key processes.

Process Flow

If we take a group of level 3 or level 4 processes and link them together, it might look something like Figures 7.5 and 7.6. Then for each of the

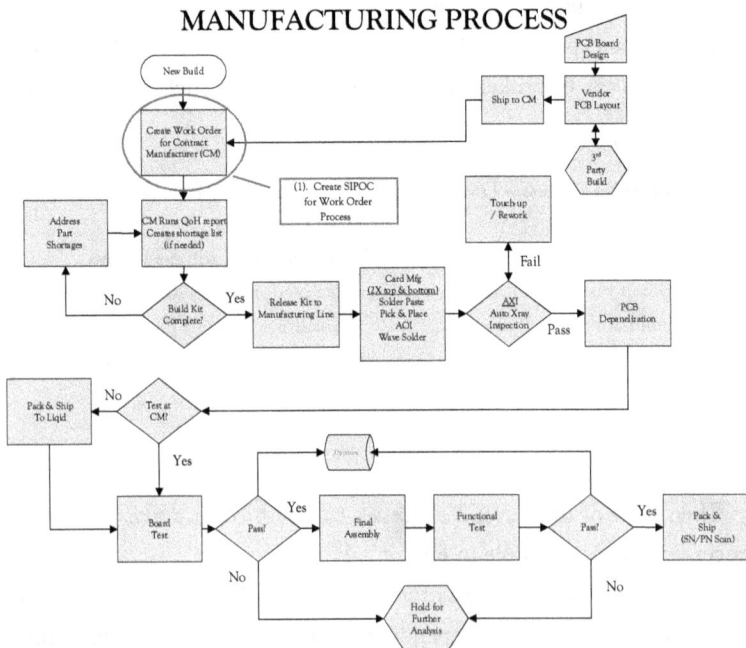

Figure 7.5 Manufacturing process

MATERIAL DISPOSITION PROCESS

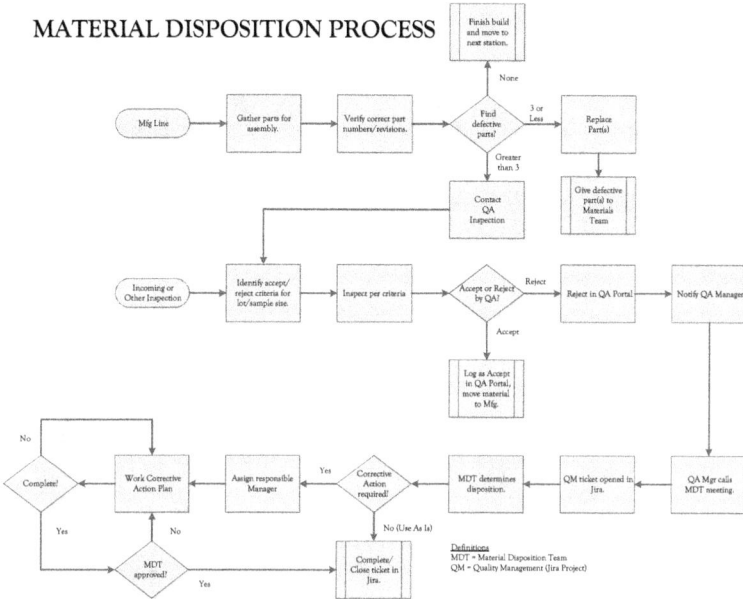

Figure 7.6 Material disposition process

blocks in the flow, you create a SIPOC. If this sounds like a lot of work, that's because it is. Documenting your processes from end to end, top to bottom is not trivial. Start with your most critical or troubled processes and address the others over time. Ultimately, if you do not have these processes documented, how are you ever going to improve them? How are you going to measure them? How will you identify the waste (*muda*)?

Process Control

Process control provides the checks and balances you put in place to ensure your process stays in control. It should be based on collecting data around a measurement or set of measurements you have put in place for your process. The measurements should help you determine if the process is running within in control, meaning within the expected amount variance. The normal variance is defined based on the control limits shown in Figure 7.7. The control limits (UCL (upper control limit) and LCL (lower control limit)) are calculated based on data collected from the process.

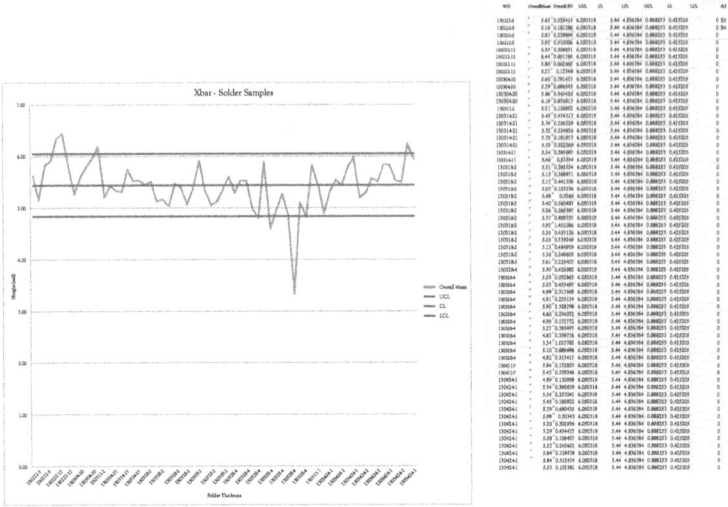

Figure 7.7 Control chart for solder samples

When points go outside the control limits, corrective action is required to bring the process back in to control.

Each functional group should know the following about their process(es):

- What are the inputs I need to complete my work?
- Who supplies them to me?
- What steps do I take to turn my inputs into an output?
- What is the output of my work?
- Who does it go to?
- How do I know if my output is meeting the requirements?
- What information can be captured to ensure I consistently meet those requirements?

For improvements you should ask:

- What is the ideal target value for my process measurement?
- What value(s) would be unacceptable?
- What steps/activities am I doing that are not absolutely necessary?
- What steps/activities should I be doing that I do not typically do?

CHAPTER 8

Data-Based Decision Making

Data Collection and Analysis

Everyone would like to make data-based decisions. In fact, why would you *not* want to use data to make decisions? But as easily as "data-based decisions" rolls off the tongue, getting real meaning out of your data does not happen without some significant effort.

Data–Information–Knowledge–Wisdom

To really make data useful, it needs to go through a transformation process. Data in its rawest form is generally not particularly useful. For example, take an output from a test run. It may barely be readable to humans. Some type of processing (parsing, organizing, sorting) needs to be done to turn it into actual information. Information provides answers, to who, what, when, and where. To move from information to knowledge, additional processing or analysis needs to take place. Knowledge is when information provides some type of conclusion or drives some type of action. Knowledge often answers question of how. Knowledge eventually becomes wisdom when it becomes understood. It drives wiser decisions.

The data–information–knowledge–wisdom model (also known as the DIKW model) is shown in Figure 8.1.

Using a methodology like GQM that we discussed earlier gives your data collection some purpose. The more specific you can be about what questions you are trying to answer, the more targeted your data collection can be. As part of your data planning, it is also important to know who your target audience is and how to customize the message to them. Figure 8.2 shows an example of laying out the data flow. In this example, the field data for return rate is compared to the goal. Drilling down into that

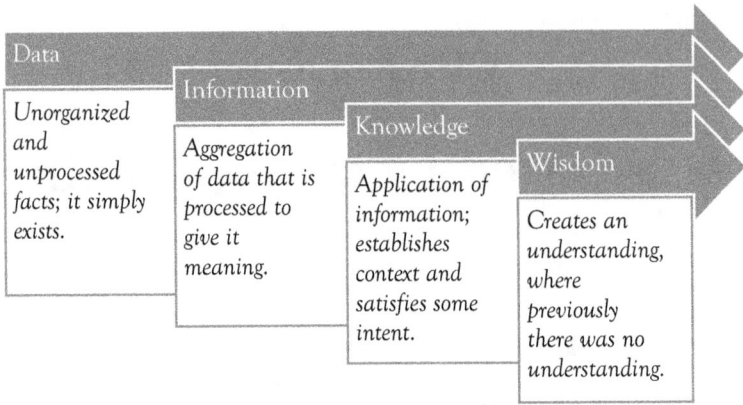

Figure 8.1 Data–information–knowledge–wisdom model

data takes different paths for management and engineering. For management, they want to understand the costs associated with those returns. For engineering, they want to understand the reason for the returns.

Data Cleansing

Depending on the source, raw data often needs to go through some type of cleansing process. If your data is not reliable, you cannot extract to the information you need. Or worse, your information may be wrong. Cleansing is a form of processing or manipulation to "scrub" the data for issues such as: incomplete records, different formats (e.g., different

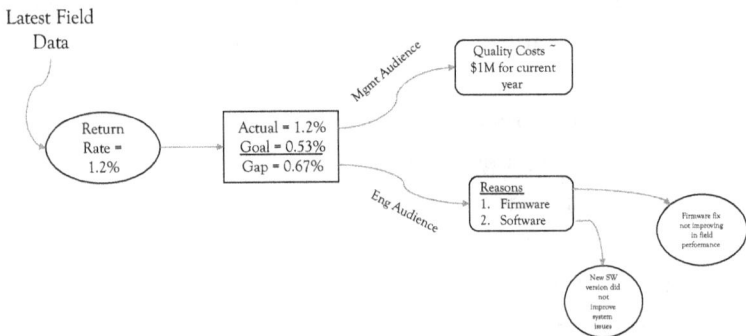

Figure 8.2 Data flow for field returns

date types), duplicate records, or mapping data from once source to another source to get the complete record. The more sophisticated your data collection system, the less cleansing you will likely need to do. But for smaller companies and new data collection efforts, the need for data cleansing is common. This work can often be automated, but the analysis team will first need to create a set of rules for how the data is checked and manipulated. Understanding the cleansing process is important to know so everyone has the right expectations. How well you manage the data cleansing will determine your level of data quality.

Data Quality

Data can originate from spread sheets, other databases, or enterprise business software. Some systems (manual or automated) allow the data to be entered in a free form, that is, the user has the freedom to enter text. An example is filling in a blank form that uses a free form text or a numeric field. These type of free-form fields, if not restricted in some way, are responsible for many errors in data reporting. This situation can occur in spreadsheets as well. Particularly when more than one person works on the same spreadsheet. Even sophisticated programs allow for free-form text fields. Whenever possible, it is recommended to the administrators of such programs that they use drop-down choices that will help ensure data integrity. Some databases can treat upper- and lower-case spellings as different fields so "Firmware," "firmware," and "firm ware" will be considered as three different values, even if it is under the same heading in a spreadsheet for example. If you are trying to display a count of 'Firmware," the fields that contain "firmware" and 'firm ware' would be missed because the database is looking for an exact match. This difference in the way data is entered or in the manner it is exported will affect accuracy and the way your project will look in a new report or dashboard. It is important that owner of the data take the time to review their work for:

- Accuracy
- Completeness
- Relevance
- Consistency from one load to another

- Reliability in its collection and format
- Free of duplications

Accuracy. Whether your data originates from a database, spreadsheet, or from another system it needs to be checked for accuracy. Spelling is one area that needs to be checked carefully. As does upper and lower case within the data fields. Misspelled words or a mix of upper and lower case will cause errors in the final presentation. Avoid abbreviations if possible. If there are issues in the data, it will be reflected in your report or dashboard.

Completeness. Check to make sure that all fields are complete and that there is consistency in the data fields. If for example, a date/time stamp is used in a report calculation and your data has some blanks in that field category, there will be inaccuracies in the final presentation. Issues can occur when any field required to do a calculation, such as Return on Investment, is left blank.

Relevance. When extracting data for use in a new report, review it from a standpoint of its relevance to the problem or issues that you are addressing. Everything else is not necessary. Try to capture only what you absolutely need.

Consistency from one load to another. When providing data for an automated report or dashboard be sure that you are providing data in exactly the same format each time. Any change, no matter how small, can affect the way the final output displays the data. For example, if your data is delivered in a spreadsheet and you add a column that you did not have before or changed a column name, that change can break the report automation. You must inform your analyst or database person, of an intended change well in advance of an expected publish date to allow for necessary reporting modifications.

Reliability in its collection and format. You must be consistent in the way that you collect and format your data. If you are extracting your data from a larger source, such as a customer relationship management (CRM) or enterprise resource planning (ERP) system, care should be taken to ensure that the same methodology is used each time you run the extraction. If you need to make changes to your data or its format, send sample data along with information on what has changed to reporting staff, so they can properly accommodate the change.

Free of duplications. Maintaining data quality requires going through the data periodically and scrubbing it. Typically, this involves updating it, standardizing it, and deduplicating records to create a single view of the data, even if it is stored in multiple disparate systems. There are many vendor applications on the market to make this job easier.

Data quality is critical to the process of transforming your information into a standard report or dashboard. This reporting will reflect your organization's business analytics and business intelligence capabilities. The emphasis on data quality assures trust in the data, which ultimately results in trust in the individual or team that is providing the reporting.

Sharing Data

How you present your data will determine your success in reaching your intended audience. As discussed in earlier chapters, one of the keys to achieving sustainable quality is to consistently keep everyone informed on your progress. Your best chance of keeping everyone updated must be as painless and hassle-free as possible. So, consider the options:

1. You can send out a weekly report through e-mail.
2. You can set up a page on an internal collaboration tool, where you post your latest results.
3. You can create a quality dashboard that is updated real time.

I was fortunate enough to manage a top-notch analytics team. They were able to do some amazing things with data that originally started out as a hodge-podge of disparate systems. It required a significant data cleansing effort before we had trustworthy data. We set up a central quality dashboard that everyone could access and see the latest quality data from across the company. It housed data from all the functional groups and all products. There were a few key benefits to having this centralized view of quality.

- Created a common view across product lines. Prior to the central dashboard, each product line presented their data in a slightly and sometimes conflicting manner. The dashboard allowed us to have a standard look and feel, as well as common rules for calculations and formulas.
- We built a central repository (data warehouse) where data from different sources were combined and cleaned, as mentioned above.
- Once charts/graphs were designed, they created live feeds from the data warehouse. This provided (almost) live feeds to the charts. So, you were always seeing the latest data.
- The dashboard had easy access from anywhere. So, executives that may be traveling could easily see the latest quality reporting on their phones.
- There was central control for updates and enhancements. Because the use of the dashboard continued to grow across the company, we had to put a request system in place to handle all the requests for changes and new reports. We eventually started publishing a dashboard roadmap, to keep everyone informed of when new features and releases would be coming out.

CHAPTER 9

Employee Focus

Make Them Successful

I believe a key responsibility of management is to make your people successful. In fact, a manager's success comes through their people's success. With that in mind, give them clear direction, give them the resources they need to be successful, help them work through any obstacles, and then get out of their way. It seems simple enough. But I'm always surprised by how many managers do not approach management this way. It should be the goal of every manager to help their employees end each day with a sense of accomplishment.

Clear Direction

Make sure your people have clear direction. I think clear direction gets established out of the bigger picture. Similar to how we approached processes; I believe roles, responsibilities, goals, and performance are linked up, down, and across the organization. At least they should be. When they are not, you open your business to indecision, inefficiencies, miscommunication, duplication, and conflict.

Certainly, this would need to be adapted to each business, but I envision the integration of all these activities working together as illustrated in Figure 9.1.

Roles and Responsibilities

A role is more than a title. You may have an engineer on a hardware team and an engineer on a software team. Both are called engineers, but they have vastly different roles. A person's role should answer the question, "a

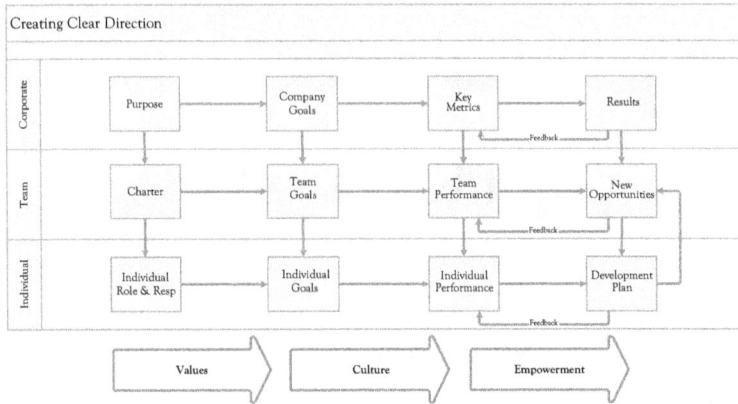

Figure 9.1 Goals and responsibilities

role in what?" Let them know how their role contributes to the department charter and the company mission. This gives them purpose. From there, you should define their responsibilities. Do not confuse tasks with responsibilities. If a person understands what they are responsible for and they have the needed skills and resources, they should be able to determine the tasks. This is exactly where empowerment comes into play. Empowerment to me is when the person has the knowledge and experience to get the job done, along with enough maturity to know when to ask for help.

Development Plan

Every individual should have a development plan. This applies to your top performers as well as your low performers. This does not mean you need to send them to expensive classes or conferences. There are many ways to develop people. Let them work with a more experienced person. Encourage them with some stretch goals, by giving them a few new responsibilities to see how they handle it. Do some mentoring/coaching in areas they need help with. The development plan should be based on the skills required for the individual's role they are in and what you think their next steps might be. It is important to keep a balance between the employee's personal growth and the department goals. The development plan should help toward both. An example development plan is shown in Figure 9.2.

Two Parts

Individual Development Plan

Performance Plan & Development Plan

Name :   Employee Number :
Dept. Mgr. :   Function/Dept :
Job Title :   Date of Hire :
Last Review :   Next review date :

Revision History:
[Date]   [revision description]

1.0 Roles and Responsibilities-
     1.1   Individual Goals
           1.1.1 Goal 1:

           1.1.2 Goal 2:

           1.1.3 Goal 3:

           1.1.4 Goal 4:

           1.1.5 Goal 5:

2.0 Factors Affecting Performance   Development Needs
     2.1 Interpersonal Communication
     2.2 Teamwork
     2.3 Technical Competence
     2.4 Additional Factor (to be chosen by employee)

Summary
3.0 Education
     3.1 B.S. Computer Science: School Name

     3.2 M.S. Computer Science   School Name

4.0 Career Goals & Aspirations
     4.1 1-2 Years: Promotion to Senior Development Engineer

     4.2 3-5 Years: Project Management

5.0 Development Plan (i.e., experience or education needed to improve current skills or support
     opportunity for career growth)

Skills Checklist & Training Plan

Skill	Supporting Experience & training	Related role & responsibility (specific goal)	Training required?	Training plan and actual dates (target) / actual

I understand that developing and implementing this plan will assist me in the
attainment of my personal career objectives but is not a guarantee of future
promotion or advancement.

Signatures:
Employee: _____ Date: _____

Manager: _____ Date: _____

Figure 9.2 Development plan

Individual Goals

Each employee should have well defined goals. As the manager, you need something measurable to provide feedback on the areas they are strong and the areas they need to improve. If you do not have a good set of goals defined, how do you assess their performance? I have had other managers tell me, "well, I know how they are doing by watching them." Here is the problem with that statement. What you have in your head as expectations, may be slightly different or even completely different than what the employee has in their head. When it comes time for the employee's review, they might be shocked at what you tell them they need to improve on. So, where you had an opportunity to inspire and motivate an employee, you have now caused frustration and demotivation. An individual goal should be linked to a team goal or department goal. If not, then why is it a goal? Help them understand how they are part of the bigger picture. This not only gives them a sense of purpose; it gives them a sense of accomplishment once the goal has been achieved.

Manager–Employee Relationship

I believe a development plan and goals have significantly more meaning when you get to know your employees. That is not necessarily a personal relationship with each person, but you should know them professionally.

What truly motivates them? Is it money? Is it a promotion? Is it a technical challenge? Every person is different. So, as you create a development plan and set goals for them, it helps to understand the person. I realize that is much easier to do when you have five people reporting to you than when you have fifty. But even when you have a large group, you can create opportunities to build a relationship.

I had the good fortune to work for a vice president that I considered a friend and mentor. He had a large organization and knew everyone that worked for him. He was always outgoing and would not pass them in the hall without asking how they are and what they were up to. Everyone loved him. He made them feel like they had a personal connection with him. Since I had a good-sized organization myself, I also want to be connected to my people. But I used a slightly different approach. I really worked at getting to know the managers that reported directly to me first. I wanted to understand what motivated them and what their career aspirations were. For the areas I could mentor or coach them, I did. For the areas I thought there might be a better alternative, I found the right mentor or training to help them. As a group, I met with the managers regularly to work through the issues, improvements, and plan for the future. We worked as a team, with everyone having an equal voice. When it came to getting to know the people in their groups, I had to create opportunities. So, I sat in each manager's staff meeting at least once a month. I didn't present or preach. I just listened, observed, and answered questions when they had them. Initially, there was some uneasiness with me sitting in their staff meeting. After a few times, the meetings became more comfortable (for them and for me) and I got the know the personalities of each team. But to go a step further, we started another initiative we jokingly called "take your boss to work day." This is where I would periodically go sit beside one of the individual contributors for a couple of hours and catch a glimpse of what their typical workday looked like. This really helped me get to know the people in my group, plus kept me very informed of the day to day activities and what issues they struggled with. These approaches helped me to build some great relationships, with some of the team eventually following me on to new adventures.

Even though my vice president and I used different approaches, they both worked to build those relationships. Think back to earlier discussions on demotivation. Most people that leave companies, quit their boss not the job. As their manager, they need to know you before they like you and like you before they trust you.

Recruiting

Getting the top technical talent available is important. But you need to balance the technical skills with the personal characteristics that fit with your team. Are the technical skills worth potentially risking the synergy within your team? What about working relationships with other groups? If your technical expert alienates others to the point that nobody wants to work with him or her, what have you gained?

If you want to build or maintain the right culture, you must look for it during your hiring process. If you use a structured interview approach, you can still emphasize the technical skills, assess their team skills, and have a scorecard that measures both. Many job descriptions are written more specifically around responsibilities. So, for the person helping with the interview, the actual skills required may be somewhat vague. A structured interview allows the hiring manager to clearly identify all the key skills they are looking for, with a weighted score for each. Here are a few benefits from using this type of approach:

- Everyone on your interview team is working from the same list of skills and can develop their own set of questions accordingly.
- Every candidate gets questioned on the same list of skills, providing a good comparison of interviewer assessments.
- Scoring is done immediately after the interview and sent to the hiring manager.
- The list of skills keeps everyone on track with their questions and the weighting helps them determine which areas to focus on in more detail.
- Because the skills are weighted and scored, it is easy to roll up the final scorecards from the interview team.
- The scoring helps to make a typically intangible process a bit more tangible.

Candidate Name: Candidate 1	Interview Date:			
Position: Data Analyst	Requisition No.: 549252			
Interviewer: Interviewer 1	Rating: 5=Very Strong 4=Above Target 3=Target 2=Below Target 1=Very Weak			

		Weighting 100 = total	Rating	Score
	Technical Skills			
1	Optimize performance of reports & queries	10	5	50
2	Ability to write & troubleshoot SQL code	10	3	30
3	Database Adminstration experience	5	2	10
4	Scripting Knowledge (Perl, PHP, Python)	5	4	20
5	General system adminstration experience (Linux, Windows)	5	3	15
6	Experience with Business Intelligence applications	5	2	10
7	Experience with web technologies	5	4	20
8	Familiarity with Statistics Packages	5	3	15
	General Skills			
1	Adaptability	5	4	20
2	High energy	5	5	25
3	Innovation	5	3	15
4	Initiative	5	4	20
5	Oral/Written Communication skills	5	3	15
	Team Skills			
1	Interpersonal & Negotiation Skills	5	4	20
2	Planning & Organizing Skills	5	3	15
3	Team Collaboration	10	5	50
4	Decision Making Approach	5	3	15
Totals		100	60	365

Figure 9.3 Individual structured interview

An example for a single interviewer is shown in Figure 9.3 and a rollup of multiple interviewers shown in Figure 9.4.

Candidate Name: Candidate 1	Interview Date:						
Position: Data Analyst	Requisition No.: 549252						
Interviewer: All	Rating: 5=Very Strong 4=Above Target 3=Target 2=Below Target 1=Very Weak						

		Weighting 100 = total	Intvw 1 Rating	Intvw 2 Rating	Intvw 3 Rating	Intvw 4 Rating	Sum Rating	Weighted Score
	Technical Skills							
1	Optimize performance of reports & queries	10	5	4	3	2	14	140
2	Ability to write & troubleshoot SQL code	10	3	2	1	3	9	90
3	Database Adminstration experience	5	2	2	2	2	8	40
4	Scripting Knowledge (Perl, PHP, Python)	5	4	4	4	4	16	80
5	General system adminstration experience (Linux, Windows)	5	3	5	3	2	13	65
6	Experience with Business Intelligence applications	5	2	3	4	1	10	50
7	Experience with web technologies	5	4	4	4	4	16	80
8	Familiarity with Statistics Packages	5	3	2	4	2	11	55
	General Skills							
1	Adaptability	5	4	5	5	4	18	90
2	High energy	5	5	5	5	5	20	100
3	Innovation	5	3	2	3	2	10	50
4	Initiative	5	4	4	4	4	16	80
5	Oral/Written Communication skills	5	3	4	3	4	14	70
	Team Skills							
1	Interpersonal & Negotiation Skills	5	4	2	4	3	13	65
2	Planning & Organizing Skills	5	3	3	3	3	12	60
3	Team Collaboration	10	5	5	4	5	19	190
4	Decision Making Approach	5	3	2	3	2	10	50
Totals		100	60	58	59	52	229	1355
							Avg Score:	338.75

Figure 9.4 Team structured interview

CHAPTER 10

Team Focus

Importance of Teams

Most work that is done in companies is done through teams. Teams are about people working together to accomplish something such as a goal, a project, and solving a problem. Some teams are short-lived, such a project team that dissolves once the project is complete. Some teams are ongoing like a department within an organization.

Benefits:

- Different perspectives
- Different skills and experiences
- Allows you to test out ideas and get feedback
- Allows you to divide up the work

Quality Teams and Quality Circles

Within TQM, quality teams or quality circles were often used to engage people at all levels to focus on quality improvement. The idea behind the quality teams was to get the people closest to the work and issues to brainstorm possible improvements. The alternative to these types of teams is for workers to complain about a problem or issue and wait for someone to come and solve it. The intent of creating quality circles was to (1) get the people most familiar with a particular process to be involved with or even develop the solution; (2) keep a focus on quality improvement; and (3) promote pride in their work by empowering people to help make a difference. Regardless of what you call these types of teams, they can be very effective. Here are a couple of examples.

Inspection Team

At one of the startup companies I worked at, I had a small group of inspectors that checked our new product at different points throughout the manufacturing process. I had noticed that my lead inspector seemed to be losing some of the passion for her role. So, I decided to challenge her. The defect rate from our inspections were not bad; however, we had not shown much improvement over recent months. I met with her to see if she would like to lead a small team to make some improvements. Not quite sure what she was getting into, she hesitantly agreed. I asked her to select a few people from the manufacturing line to brainstorm with. Then I had her pull the defect data and helped her summarize it. I sat in the first meeting with her and the team, just help explain that we are looking for improvement ideas to drive down the defects. From there I let her run with it, helping her occasionally with charts and graphs. The team did exceptionally well. They proposed some great improvements, which we implemented. For her, there was a significant change in her attitude and enthusiasm. She really enjoyed "leading" something and embraced the opportunity. In fact, she did so well that I ended up promoting her later that year.

Cross-Functional Test Teams (CFTT)

At one of the large companies, we had a significant test effort going on. We had multiple departments working on multiple products, across multiple divisions. Unfortunately, it became very inefficient. The different groups were each doing their own type of testing, but none of it was coordinated. There were considerable overlaps where groups were repeating testing another group had previously done and did not know it. There were also gaps, where some testing was not getting done at all. As part of our reengineering effort for testing, we established a concept we called cross-functional test teams (CFTT). We created a CFTT for every product that was going through test. The CFTT was made up of representatives from each of the test groups, so each new product was assigned a coordinated team, with a cross-section of testing skills. We used requirements-based testing (RBT) to divide up the work, so we eliminated gaps and overlaps. For each CFTT, we identified a CFTT lead. The CFTT lead was basically a technical program manager that managed and coordinated the entire test effort for the end-to-end test effort. This concept became a highly effective way of focusing teams to improve their test coverage. So much so that we built this concept into our overall test strategy. We developed a selection process for CFFT leads and used it as a training ground for future program managers and test managers.

Importance of Roles and Responsibilities

One of the keys to making the CFTT concept successful was to have clear roles and responsibilities. Without this understanding, it is easy to fall into the gaps and overlaps problem. Knowing the roles and responsibilities of each member is important for any team whether it is members of the same department or members of a cross-functional team. Once each individual knows what is expected of them, they have a sense of purpose and their job becomes more meaningful.

Recognizing Unproductive Teams

A first step to recognizing unproductive teams is to go back to how the team was originally put together. Were there tight relationships between some members before joining the team? Was there animosity between certain members before joining the team? Did members get assigned to the team or did they volunteer? In the case of a departmental team, were previous team members involved in the selection process? Understanding the background of how the team was constructed could provide clues to the current behavior. When watching the team operate, here are some indicators that they may have become unproductive:

- Increased complaining
- More excuses
- Failure to share information
- Communication breakdowns
- Lack of trust among members
- Small silos within the team

- General lack of respect for each other
- Workload imbalances
- Not taking responsibility
- Looking for scapegoats
- Continued or increasing conflict

Building High-Performance Teams

A company I was working for came up with a breakthrough product that was expected to leapfrog the competition and boost our revenues. There was a serious commitment to making this new product a success. The entire team, engineering, test, marketing, manufacturing, support would all be co-located together. I was asked to put together an elite test team. I was given approval to take whomever I wanted from any test group to build this team. I quickly realized that this team was going to be spending some significant time together, as well as working very closely with the engineering teams. So, I really wanted to build a "team" and not just a group of experts. I did select some of the top test engineers from various groups, putting together the complimentary skills we would need. But I did not comprise on the "team" aspect, making sure to select engineers that had demonstrated they were team players and had a reputation for working well with others. The team came together better than I could have hoped, and we quickly developed a great working relationship with the engineering team. Our test team became known as the "Dream Team" and I had test engineers approach me quite often about joining our special group.

Our Dream Team was certainly a high-performing team. But it was high performing because we had a great balance of technical excellence and collaboration. The team genuinely enjoyed working together and helping each other be successful. It also helped that our mission was truly clear, and everyone knew what their role was in the launch of this new product. Here are some key factors for building a high-performing team:

- A clear direction and mission
- A shared set of goals

- Clear roles and responsibilities
- Leadership that leads by example and knocks down obstacles
- Respect for each other
- Healthy communication
- Challenge one another, but do not let disagreement turn into conflict
- Success as a team over success individually

Decision Making with Teams

Decisions within a team need to be made collaboratively. That does not mean that all decisions need to be unanimous. But everyone should have the opportunity to share their opinion. In fact, you want that. More ideas and perspectives are always better than one person deciding in a vacuum or deciding for others. When all team members feel they have an opportunity to contribute toward a decision, everyone's roles are clear, they care for one another, and they are all working toward a common goal, you have likely created a high-performing team.

CHAPTER 11

Reward and Recognition

When it comes to employees, most businesses utilize some type of reward and recognition. First, let us look at the difference between reward and recognition. A reward is usually something tangible, like a gift or a sum of money. Recognition can happen anytime. It can be as simple as a manager telling an employee they did a great job on their report.

But I have always though that reward and recognition is a delicate thing for management. In many cases, they can result in more negatives than positives, in my opinion. If you have 50 people and you reward 5 of them, you may have motivated the 5, but there are 45 that may not feel the same way. And if you consistently tell an employee they did a great job, after a while, they will begin to wonder when the recognition turns into a reward of some type. Depending on how these programs are implemented, it could create some bad behaviors. Recognizing employees in front of their peers is a double-edged sword. You can create behavior where a few may want to win at all costs, just to get that recognition. I have seen this play out where employees take credit for another employee's work. Or, they make another employee look bad, so they can look good.

I am not trying to say reward and recognition is bad. In fact, I absolutely believe employees should be rewarded and recognized. I just think some serious thought needs to go into how you implement it. Exactly what behaviors do you want to reward? If it is employees that go "above and beyond," then clearly define "above and beyond" and the rules of the game. However the rules are defined, everyone should have an equal chance to achieve them.

Focus on Teams

I have always felt that rewarding teamwork is much more effective than individual rewards. If most of your work is done in teams, why not reward and recognize them as a team? This way you are not picking one person to single out and demotivating the rest of the team that likely helped them. If the behaviors you are looking for are teamwork, collaboration, and inclusiveness, then give employees an incentive to do more of that.

When I was working with the dream team, the head of engineering approached me and asked if we could do something together to recognize our teams. Both teams had been putting in some long hours and we wanted to let them know we appreciated it. We thought about handing out gift certificates or something similar. Then he asked me, "what if we just take them out for a few drinks and a few snacks and let them get to know each other better?" I liked that idea. We found a place near by the office that had room to move around and mingle. We ordered some drinks and appetizers. Then we just let them talk and spend some time together in a relaxed setting. The whole evening ended up costing much less than gift certificates would have, plus we got much more out of it. Both teams told us how much they appreciated it. We decided to make this a monthly event over the course of the program, and it paid big dividends for us. There was a great bond between the teams. When issues came up, there was no "them versus us." It was just friends working through those issues together.

Individual reward and recognition can still be done between the manager and employee. Having regular reviews with each employee is intended to provide the feedback and the recognition they need. This is also an opportunity to reward them if they have done well. The reward can not only be a pay increase, it could include increased responsibilities, a promotion, or new opportunities.

This is not to say the individual reward and recognition should never happen publicly. There are always *exceptions*. When an individual does something so outstanding that everyone recognizes it, then certainly they should be singled out. But that should be the exception and not the rule. When everyone is getting rewards, it becomes watered down and loses much of the meaning.

How Recognition Programs Support New Model

By recognizing teams, you reinforce the behaviors you want to see more of. If we tie this back to our sustaining quality model, we want employees to continuously be thinking—"how do I make this better?" If whatever recognition you are providing makes them feel appreciated and valued, they will be much more likely to keep improving. Whether it is a cross-functional team or a departmental team, recognizing them together strengthens the bond between them. Give them the opportunities to build trust with each other. Once they begin to help and support each other, it becomes more about "we" than "I." When that happens, your team is performing at another level.

CHAPTER 12

Continuous Improvement

The New Process Improvement Process

The model we covered in Chapter 3 describes the general approach to sustainable quality. We start by building a culture of quality as the foundation for sustained change. Then we clearly define our vision, goals, and measurements. Then we use the tools and methods to develop and implement the improvements.

But to achieve "sustainable quality," it requires continuous improvement, which means continuous reevaluation. The new model provides an approach for a companywide transformation, often triggered by a significant change. These larger changes can come from external forces, such as competition, the economy, or technology, as well as from internal conditions, such as mergers, acquisitions, business constraints, or new systems.

However, incremental changes occur across a company which may not be as widespread. This might include reorganizations, new departments, growing workforce, or new programs. These smaller changes may be happening at different times and for different durations. When groups begin to meet their goals, or incremental changes occur, they should continue to look for opportunities where additional improvements can be made.

To that end, there is a process that builds off the model in Chapter 3. I call it the sustainable quality improvement (SQI) process. This process is shown in Figure 12.1.

The SQI process follows the approach used in Chapter 3 but is streamlined to be an extension of the new model for incremental improvements. This process is intended to follow the initial improvement effort to maintain the emphasis on continuous improvement.

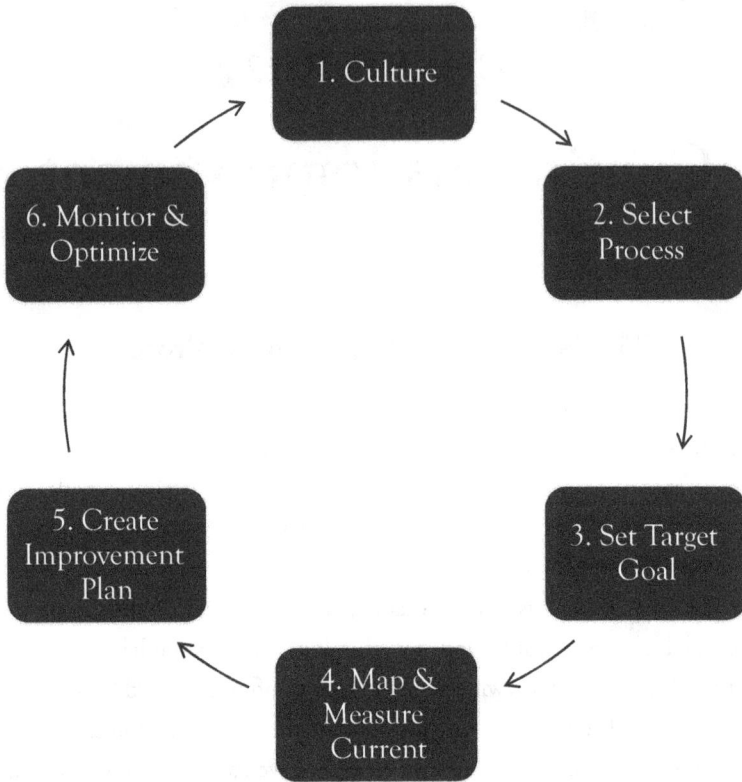

Figure 12.1 SQI process

1. *Assess the Culture.* Assess or reassess the culture for its readiness to change. Have there been changes from internal or external forces that could have an impact on the culture? Are there new barriers or issues that need to be addressed before introducing change?
2. *Process Selection.* Determine the highest priority process(es) needing improvement. Utilize cost of quality to identify priorities, based on actual costs in dollars. Focus on the processes with the highest cost of poor quality. In priority order, you should focus on:
   (a) External failure costs
   (b) Internal failure costs
   (c) Appraisal costs
3. *Set Goals (Future State).* Set target goals/metrics for these processes. Use GQM to establish meaningful goals and metrics.

4. *Map and Measure (Current State)*. Map and document the current processes "as is." Establish the current metrics to set your baseline in the "as is" state.

5. *Create and Implement Improvement Plan (Action)*. You need to understand the current state, future state, and what the gap is. Develop a plan to close the gap between current state and target goals. Utilize the appropriate tools and methods that were described in Chapter 3.

6. *Monitor and Optimize*. Put the appropriate measures and controls in place to optimize the process. Is there wasted steps that can be removed? Are there ways to reduce costs or improve throughput?

7. *Start Over*. As you went through your selection process in step 2, you should have created a prioritized list of opportunities based on quality costs. Using that same list, you can move on with the next process in your prioritized list.

Why This Is Different

There is no shortage of improvement processes available to choose from. But what I think makes the SQI process different from others are three distinct factors:

1. *Assessing the culture*. For change to be sustained, you must have a culture that supports it. Since nothing ever stays the same, keeping a pulse on the culture at various levels, ensures you will maintain an environment that continues to embrace change and care about improvement.

2. *Selecting the right processes*. Selection should be determined by the one metric that matters most—money. Using cost of quality (CoQ) as the selection criteria makes it tangible and quantifiable. This also creates a direct link between your business and your improvement efforts.

3. *Setting meaningful goals*. Using a structured approach to setting goals allows you to challenge the team without being unrealistic. The methods explained in Chapter 3, such as GQM, provide that structure. There should be a linkage between lower level goals (i.e., individual contributors) and higher level goals (i.e., senior

management). You also need to have a connection between your goals and the supporting metrics, to ensure you are tracking to plan.

Benefits

Using the SQI process, you can *sustain* a continuous focus on improvement. This is the "continuous" part of continuous improvement. By using this approach, you can realize the following benefits:

- Keep people engaged and focused on quality
- Maintain a pulse on your culture by heading off resistance and preventing it from slipping back to an older state
- Continued cost reductions
- Improved decisions based on data
- Improved empowerment
- Improved productivity
- Improved team performance
- Continued progress toward prevention, reducing appraisal and failures costs

Tracking Your Progress

As you continue your improvement journey, you will want to monitor your progress, At the highest level, continued investment in prevention will add to your overall total cost of quality. But if that investment results in dramatically lowering the costs for appraisal, internal and external failures, then the total cost of quality will go down. The example in Figure 12.2 shows the prevention costs increasing, but the total cost of quality (blue line) going down.

If you recall from the beginning of this book, there was an example where the cost of poor quality was 30 percent. However, if improvements are made, through investments in prevention, the impact can be seen as shown in Figure 12.3. This shows the cost of poor quality going below 10 percent in year 4. While this is just an example, it illustrates how investing in prevention can drive down the cost of poor quality.

Total Cost of Quality by Quarter

	Year 1	Year 2	Year 3	Year 4
Prevention	$8,500	$13,500	$26,250	$38,200
Appraisal	$19,400	$31,250	$39,500	$38,000
Internal Fail	$1,264,500	$817,000	$322,500	$149,500
External Fail	$1,055,000	$783,000	$647,000	$401,000
Total Cost of Quality	$2,347,400	$1,644,750	$1,035,250	$626,700

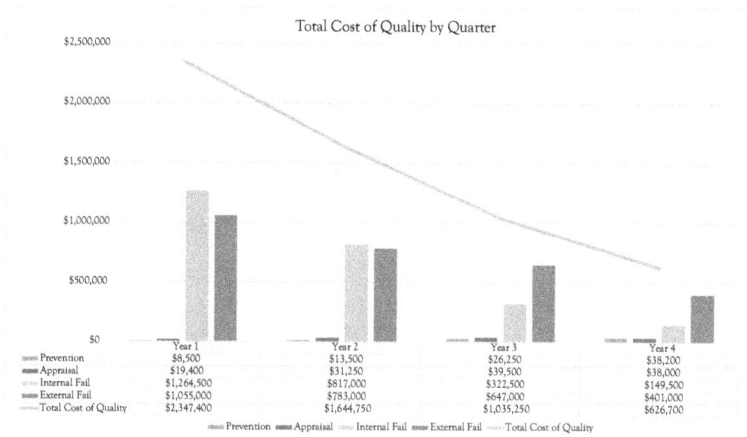

Figure 12.2 Prevention costs

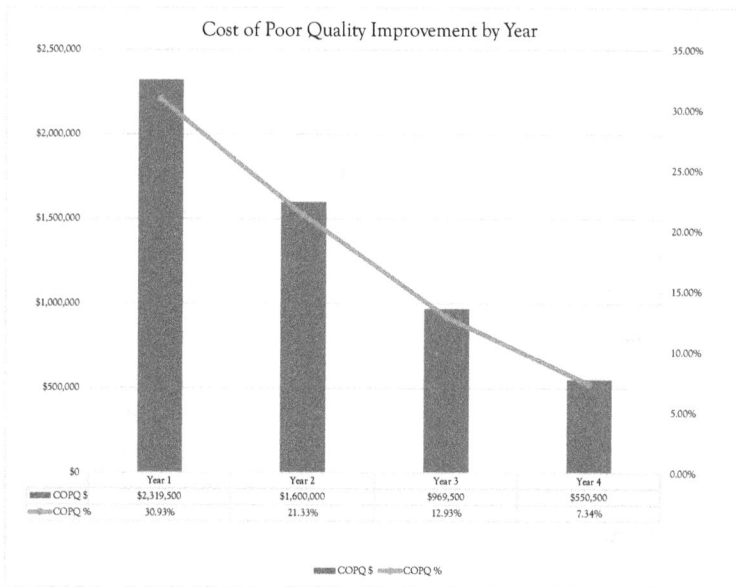

Cost of Poor Quality Improvement by Year

	Year 1	Year 2	Year 3	Year 4
COPQ $	$2,319,500	$1,600,000	$969,500	$550,500
COPQ %	30.93%	21.33%	12.93%	7.34%

Year	Year 1	Year 2	Year 3	Year 4
Revenues	$7,500,000	$7,500,000	$7,500,000	$7,500,000
COPQ %	30.93%	21.33%	12.93%	7.34%
COPQ $	$2,319,500	$1,600,000	$969,500	$550,500

Figure 12.3 Poor quality costs

Conclusion

Certainly, there are the technical aspects of a quality improvement effort, such as defining metrics, data analysis, determining root cause, and implementing improvements. Hopefully, this book provided some insight to those within the different functional groups and in the areas of focus. The intent was to paint a picture of how quality touches all areas of a business. Each function has a role and responsibility in the overall improvement. However, the collective participation of this effort is what makes it powerful and effective.

But when it comes down to it, sustainable quality is about people. Continuous improvement requires ongoing change. Change happens through people. As a leader, you must be prepared to set the stage for change. This is best achieved by creating an environment where people feel valued and are given the guidance and support, they need to flourish. It is about developing a shared vision that inspires and creates meaning in the day-to-day work of the organization. People align through common purpose, much like a sports team, where each team member is focused on the common goal of winning a championship.

For quality improvement to be embraced across the workforce, it must become internalized. It is more than an awareness. It needs to align with their values. Peter Senge[1] said that when the connection develops between what really matters in your life and what you are doing professionally, work takes on a different meaning.

But how do you get a workforce to develop this intrinsic meaning of quality? The inside-out approach mentioned earlier from Covey[2] eventually manifests itself as pride. When this happens, you have successfully created an environment where people feel excited about coming to work. That excitement and that internal desire to improve is maintained through a culture of quality. When individually and collectively people feel connected to your success, great things can happen. You will know when that drive to continuously get better becomes internalized. Because you will no longer need to ask for improvement projects. They will flow out of the workforce naturally.

---

[1] Senge (1990).
[2] Covey (1992).

Bibliography

Alansohn, A, B. Derksen, A. Engels, M. Hardy, E. Kvaalen, D.J. Leivick, A. Liefting, C. Markel, C. Matthews, R. Charles, Chris, et al. 2012. "Six Sigma and Quality Management." *MBA Student Text.* http://6sigma.weebly.com/uploads/1/2/0/7/120786/six_sigma_learning_book.pdf (accessed on July 23, 2020).

Basili, V.R. 1992. *Software Modeling and Measurement: The Goal/Question/Metric Paradigm*, 1–24. Digital Repository at the University of Maryland.

Bodnarczuk, M. October 2006. "Why Organizational Culture Matters." *Breckenridge Institute*, pp. 10–12.

Crosby, P.B. 1979. *Quality is Free: The Art of Making Quality Certain.* New York, NY: McGraw-Hill, Inc.

Gitlow, H.S., and S.J. Gitlow. 1987. *The Deming Guide to Quality and Competitive Position.* Englewood Cliffs, New Jersey: Prentice Hall, Inc.

Humphrey, W. 2008. "The Software Quality Challenge." *Crosstalk-The Journal of Defense Software Engineering, Standish Group, Chaos Report*, pp. 4–9.

INCOSE. August 2007. *Systems Engineering handbook: A Guide for System Life Cycle Processes and Activities v3.1.* Hoboken, New Jersey: John Wiley & Sons.

Juran, and Crosby. February 28, 1990. "A Note on Quality: The Views of Deming." *Harvard Business Review* 9-687-022, pp. 1–14.

Juran, J.M. 1951. *Quality Control Handbook.* 3rd ed. New York, NY: McGraw-Hill, Inc.

Krasner, H. September 2018. "The Cost of Poor Quality Software in the US: A 2018 Report." *CISQ Consortium for IT Software Quality.* p. 5.

Lyu, M.R. 1996. *Handbook of Software Reliability Engineering - Chapter 9 - ODC.* New York, NY: Computer Society Press and McGraw-Hill Book Company.

Okkenburg, A. June 04, 2012. "Agile vs. Waterfall – Why not both". *IT405, IFET College of Engineering.*

Research History. 2012. "Maslow's Hierarchy of Needs." *A Theory of Human Motivation, A. H. Maslow, Hierarchy of Needs, Self-Actualization.* http://researchhistory.org/2012/06/16/maslows-hierarchy-of-needs/?print=1 (accessed on July 16, 2020).

Sarah, T., and W. Noel. 2018. "Tricentis Software Fail Watch Finds 3.6 Billion People Affected and $1.7 Trillion Revenue Lost by Software Failures Last Year." https://tricentis.com/news/tricentis-software-fail-watch-finds-3-6-billion-people-affected-and-1-7-trillion-revenue-lost-by-software-failures-last-year/ (accessed on July 21, 2020).

Senge, P.S. 1990. *The Fifth Discipline: The Art and Practice of The Learning Organization*. New York, NY: Doubleday/Currency.

Shep, H. 2015. "Drucker Said 'Culture Eats Strategy For Breakfast'," *Drucker Said 'Culture Eats Strategy For Breakfast' and Enterprise Rent-A-Car Proves It*. https://forbes.com/sites/shephyken/2015/12/05/drucker-said-culture-eats-strategy-for-breakfast-and-enterprise-rent-a-car-proves-it/#6f69a05c2749 (accessed on July 16, 2020).

Stephen, R.C. 1994. "A Total Approach to Total Quality." *Total Quality Stephen R. Covey*. https://bhushanborntowin.wordpress.com/2006/12/29/total-quality-stephen-r-covey/ (accessed on July 16, 2020).

Stratton. D.A. 1994. *A Quality Transformation Success Story from StorageTek*. Milwaukee, WI: ASQC Quality Press.

Tassey, G., Ph.d, prepared by RTI. May 2002. *The Economic Impacts of Inadequate Infrastructure for Software Testing*. Final Report. pp. ES-3.

Tobius, P.A., and D.C. Trindade. 1995. *Applied Reliability*, 2nd ed. New York, NY: Chapman & Hall.

Tom, S. 2013. "Product/Market Expansion Matrix." *Product/Market Expansion Matrix*. https://spencertom.com/2013/10/09/ansoff-matrix/#U60YwZSSz3Q (accessed on July 16, 2020).

Whittaker, J., J. Arbon., and J. Carollo. 2012. *How Google Tests Software*. Upper Saddle River, New Jersey: Pearson Education Inc. and Addison-Wesley, Inc.

About the Author

Joseph Diele is a senior quality management professional with more than 25 years of experience in small and large technology companies. He is an influential leader with extensive background in the engineering disciplines of quality, reliability, and testing. Joe's proven strengths include analysis, problem solving, and management. He is known for driving positive change and improving quality. Joe has been on the cutting edge of new methods and practices and has consistently raised the level of maturity in the organizations where he has worked. Throughout his career, Joe has been well-recognized for leading transformative change and building high-performing teams. His interests include developing creative solutions for systemic problems, continuous improvement, and examining culture as it pertains to quality and operational performance. Joe has a B.S. in Information Systems and M.S. in Management, with an emphasis in leading change. He graduated both degree programs with honors. Joe is also certified as a Lean Six Sigma Black Belt.

Index

OTHER TITLES IN THE SUPPLY AND OPERATIONS MANAGEMENT COLLECTION
Joy M. Field, Boston College, Editor

- *The Cost, Volume IV* by Chris Domanski
- *The Barn Door is Open* by Serge Alfonse
- *Operations Management in China* by Craig Seidelson
- *Logistics Management* by Tan Miller, and Matthew J. Liberatore
- *The Practical Guide to Transforming Your Company* by Daniel Plung, and Connie Krull
- *Leading and Managing Strategic Suppliers* by Richard Moxham
- *Moving the Chains* by Domenico LePore
- *The New Age Urban Transportation Systems, Volume II* by Sundaravalli Narayanaswami
- *The New Age Urban Transportation Systems, Volume I* by Sundaravalli Narayanaswami
- *Optimizing the Supply Chain* by Jay E. Fortenberry
- *Insightful Quality, Second Edition* by Victor E. Sower, and Frank K. Fair
- *Managing Using the Diamond Principle* by Mark W. Johnson
- *The Effect of Supply Chain Management on Business Performance* by Milan Frankl
- *The Global Supply Chain and Risk Management* by Stuart Rosenberg
- *Moving into the Express Lane* by Rick Pay
- *Sustain* by Scott W. Culberson

Concise and Applied Business Books

The Collection listed above is one of 30 business subject collections that Business Expert Press has grown to make BEP a premiere publisher of print and digital books. Our concise and applied books are for...

- Professionals and Practitioners
- Faculty who adopt our books for courses
- Librarians who know that BEP's Digital Libraries are a unique way to offer students ebooks to download, not restricted with any digital rights management
- Executive Training Course Leaders
- Business Seminar Organizers

Business Expert Press books are for anyone who needs to dig deeper on business ideas, goals, and solutions to everyday problems. Whether one print book, one ebook, or buying a digital library of 110 ebooks, we remain the affordable and smart way to be business smart. For more information, please visit www.businessexpertpress.com, or contact sales@businessexpertpress.com.

www.ingramcontent.com/pod-product-compliance
Lightning Source LLC
Chambersburg PA
CBHW061307220326
41599CB00026B/4775